W0081414

this book belongs to

# A DATING DIARY

a journal for anyone looking
for their special someone

Lisa Currie
a TarcherPerigee book

**tarcherperigee**

an imprint of Penguin Random House LLC
penguinrandomhouse.com

Copyright © 2024 Lisa Currie
Penguin Random House supports copyright. Copyright fuels creativity,
encourages diverse voices, promotes free speech, and creates a vibrant culture.
Thank you for buying an authorized edition of this book and for complying with
copyright laws by not reproducing, scanning, or distributing any part of it in
any form without permission. You are supporting writers and allowing
Penguin Random House to continue to publish books for every reader.

TarcherPerigee with tp colophon is a registered trademark of Penguin Random House LLC

Most TarcherPerigee books are available at special quantity discounts for bulk
purchase for sales promotions, premiums, fund-raising, and educational needs.
Special books or book excerpts also can be created to fit specific needs.
For details, write: Specialmarkets@penguinrandomhouse.com.

ISBN: 9780593712689

Printed in the United States of America
1st Printing

While the author has made every effort to provide accurate telephone numbers,
Internet addresses and other contact information at the time of publication, neither
the publisher nor the author assumes any responsibility for errors, or for changes that
occur after publication. Further, publisher does not have any control over and does
not assume any responsibility for author or third-party websites or their content.

to our hopeful hearts

## 11

## DAYDREAMS

let your hopes
& hesitations out
onto the page

## 39

## REFLECTIONS

a space to untangle
where you've been
& what you want

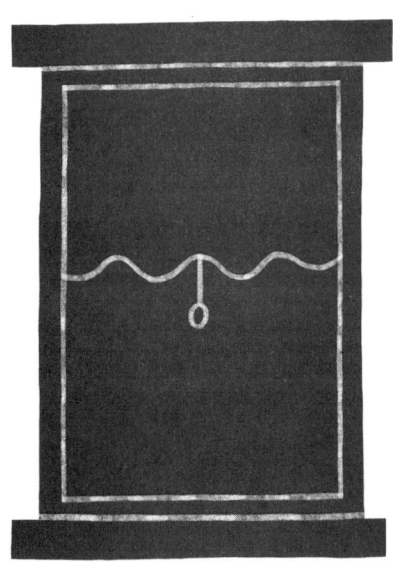

## 71

## PEP TALKS

a loving blanket to
wrap around yourself
when you need comfort
or encouragement

## 107

## SOUVENIRS

the place to go for
a debrief after you
meet someone new

# AN INTRODUCTION

when you're a single person trying to reflect on your dating life, it can get noisy quickly. there are friends eager to give you advice. couples who seem delighted to feed off your dating stories as entertainment. posts online that make you feel you're never doing enough to find love, not going about it the "right" way or even doing too much! it's a lot.

this book is a space of your own to explore love & connection while also being a soft place to land in solitude & gently untangle some of the knots in your mind. somewhere to tune in to your own innate wisdom about what you want & what feels right.

while writing this book, i happened to be
reading a biography of Tenzin Palmo,
the Buddhist nun who spent twelve years
in solitude in a cave in the Himalayas,
one of many stories about aloneness
i'm fascinated by.

it felt like a strange duality to have this
insatiable curiosity about hermits throughout
history (& in fiction!) while creating a book
about dating & the desire to find love.

when you've been single for a while, it can
feel like a comfort to proclaim it as a choice:
i don't want a relationship! i'm happy as is!
maybe that's partly why the hermit life
has felt tempting to me at times.

i realize, though, meaningful solitude is not
the whole truth of what i want. i do crave
partnership & hope to someday meet a special
someone who feels like home to me.

but how can we remain openhearted
without it overwhelming us?

the modern search for connection moves
at an anxious, relentless pace. there are
gamified dating apps in our pockets & an
overwhelming amount of choice. it's easy to
let the algorithm take the lead, but how
might we tune into our own inner rhythms?

i want to enjoy the here & now of being
single & still acknowledge it feels really lonely
sometimes. i want to keep myself open to
love without it feeling like a full-time job
to snag a partner. i want to soak up all the
love i'm lucky to have in my life right now
& still cultivate the wish for more.

from these hopes, this book was born.
i hope it can be a friend to you!

# A FEW SUGGESTIONS

take a moment (a few breaths) to sit
with each page before you rush to answer.
what you want to say might not come to you
right away. let your mind gently wander.
maybe come back to that page later on.

start at the start of the book, or just flick
to whichever page catches your eye today.
if you want to debrief after a date, then
"souvenirs" (page 107) is the place to go.

this book is yours to make your own.
you might think of it like a conversation
with the page. you can write, doodle or add
color. there's really no wrong way to go
about it. the best thing is to just begin!

# AN IMPORTANT NOTE

these pages welcome whatever pronouns you
(or the people you date) choose to use.
this book welcomes whatever sexuality you
identify with or want to explore.

i use the phrase "special someone" throughout
these pages because it feels sweet to me &
inclusive of whatever your idea of a loving
relationship or family might look like.

# LET'S BEGIN!

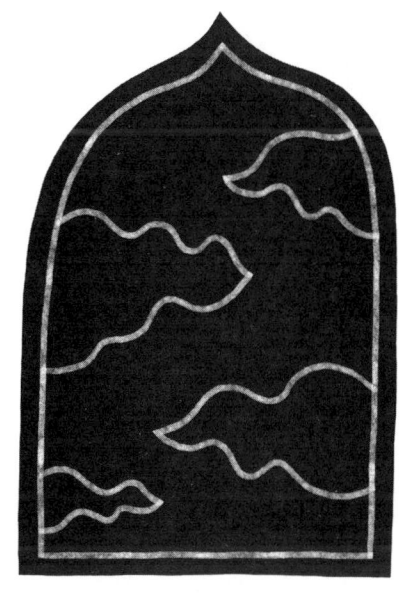

# DAYDREAMS

when i imagine a love to
thrill & consume me,
what do i see?

when i imagine a love that
burns quiet & steady,
what do i see?

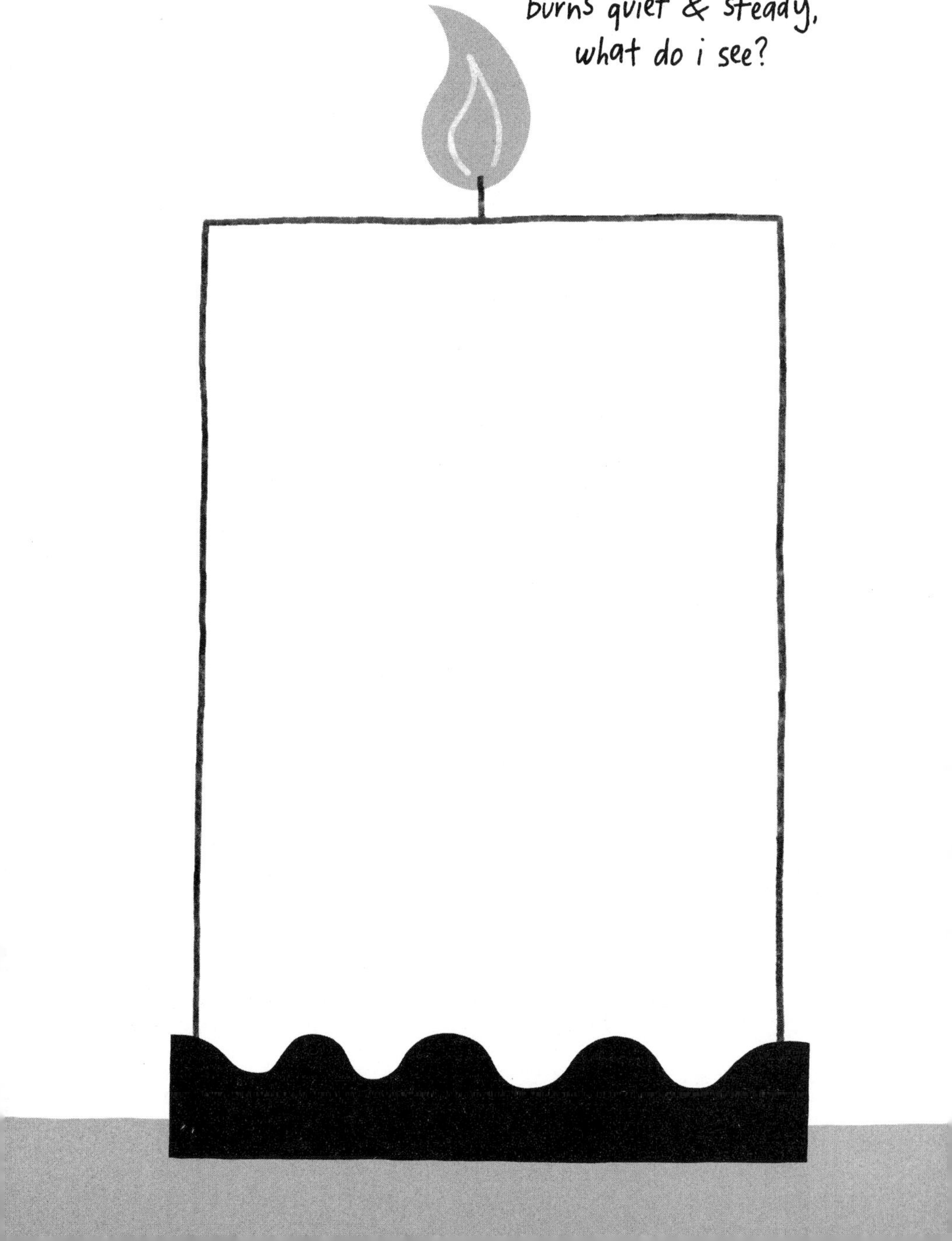

what gives me that instant spark of
lust or attraction when i meet someone?

what makes me feel safe & warm
as we get to know each other?

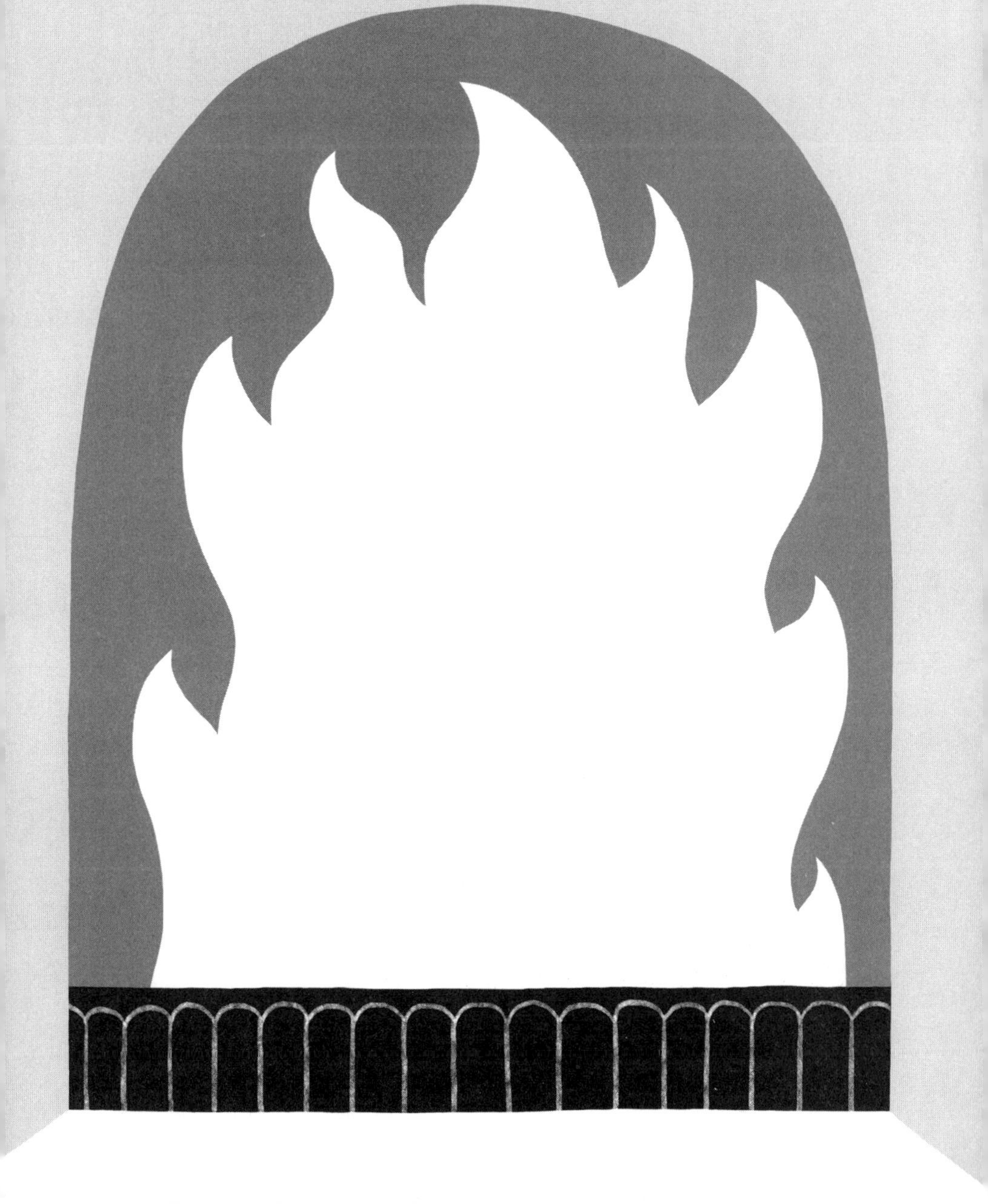

the fears or worries
i have about getting
close to someone

the parts of being in love i feel ready & excited for

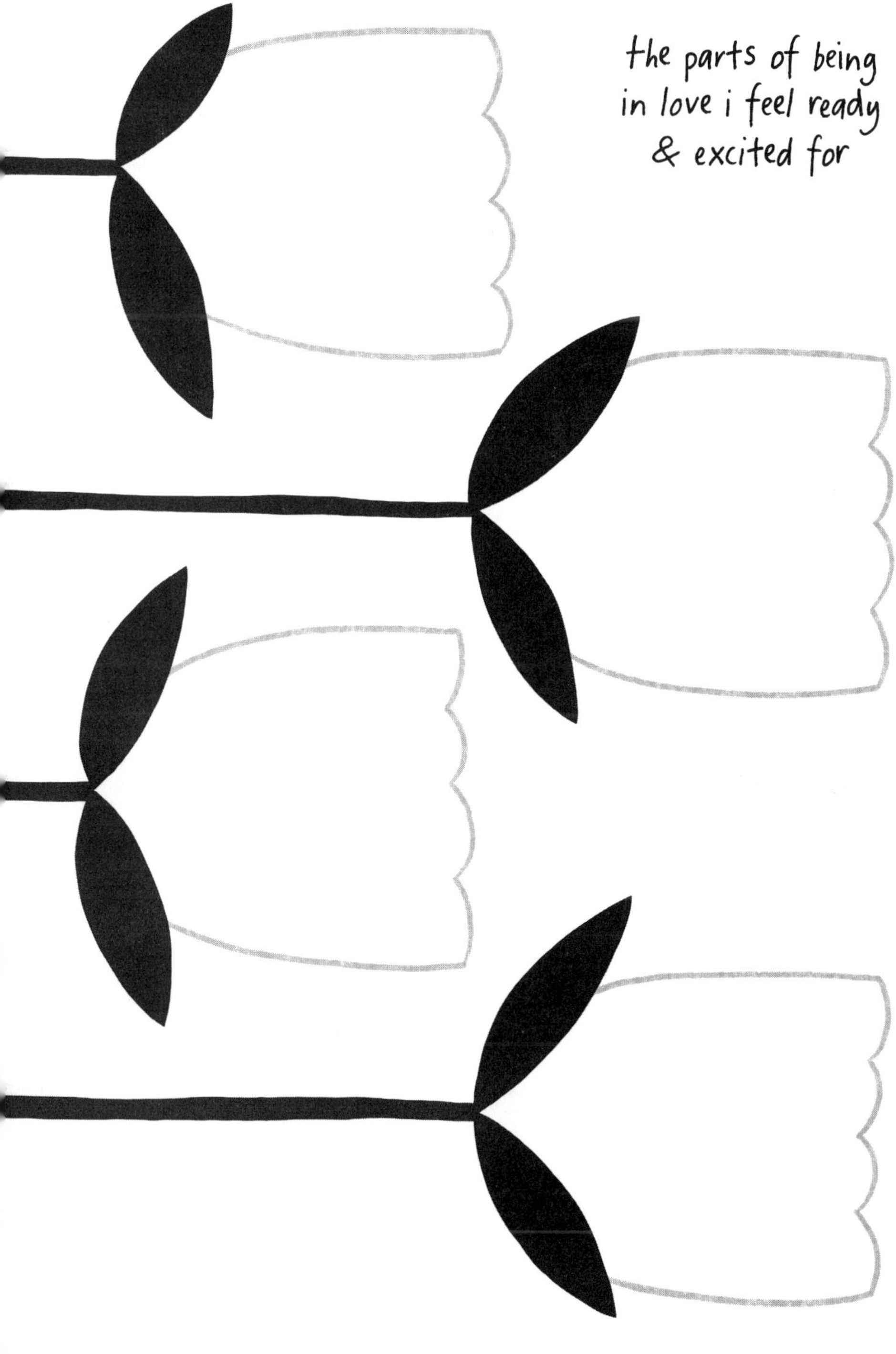

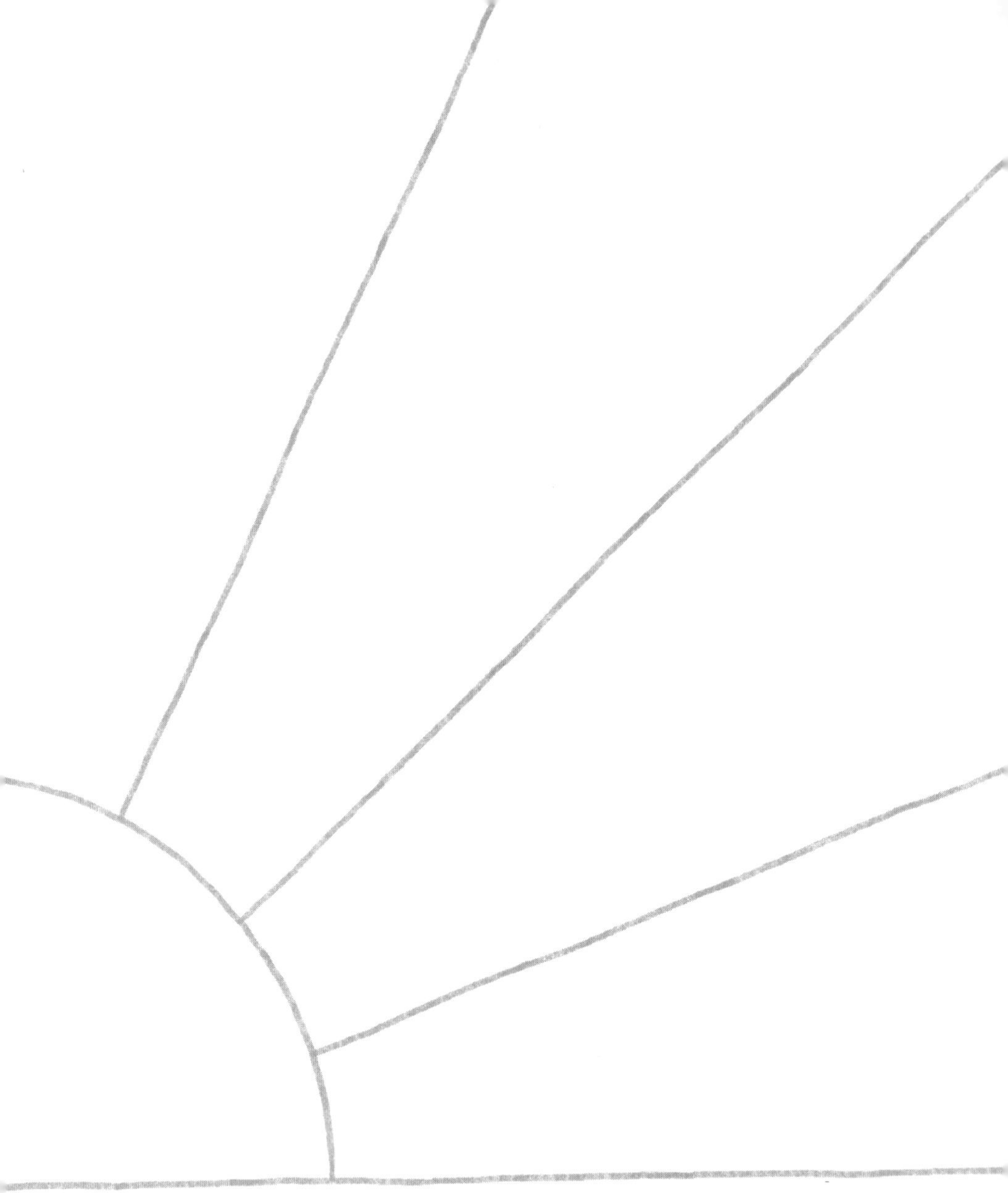

what i imagine life with a special someone
would look like – our perfectly nice but
mundane days together.

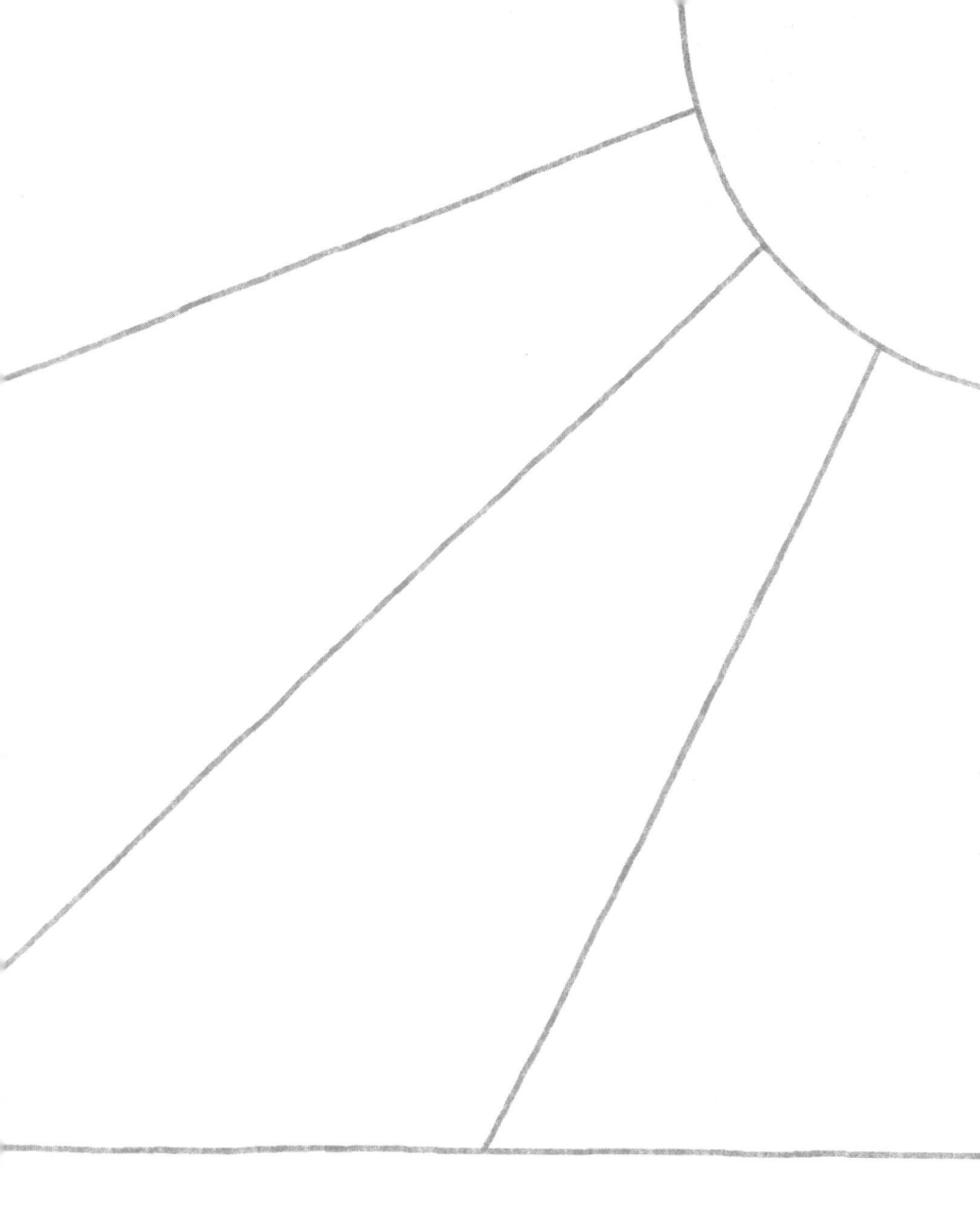

(say, a lazy Saturday, or a Tuesday
when we both have to work.)

19

aside from the way i look or things i own,
what do I have to offer a special someone?
what are the shapes of my love?

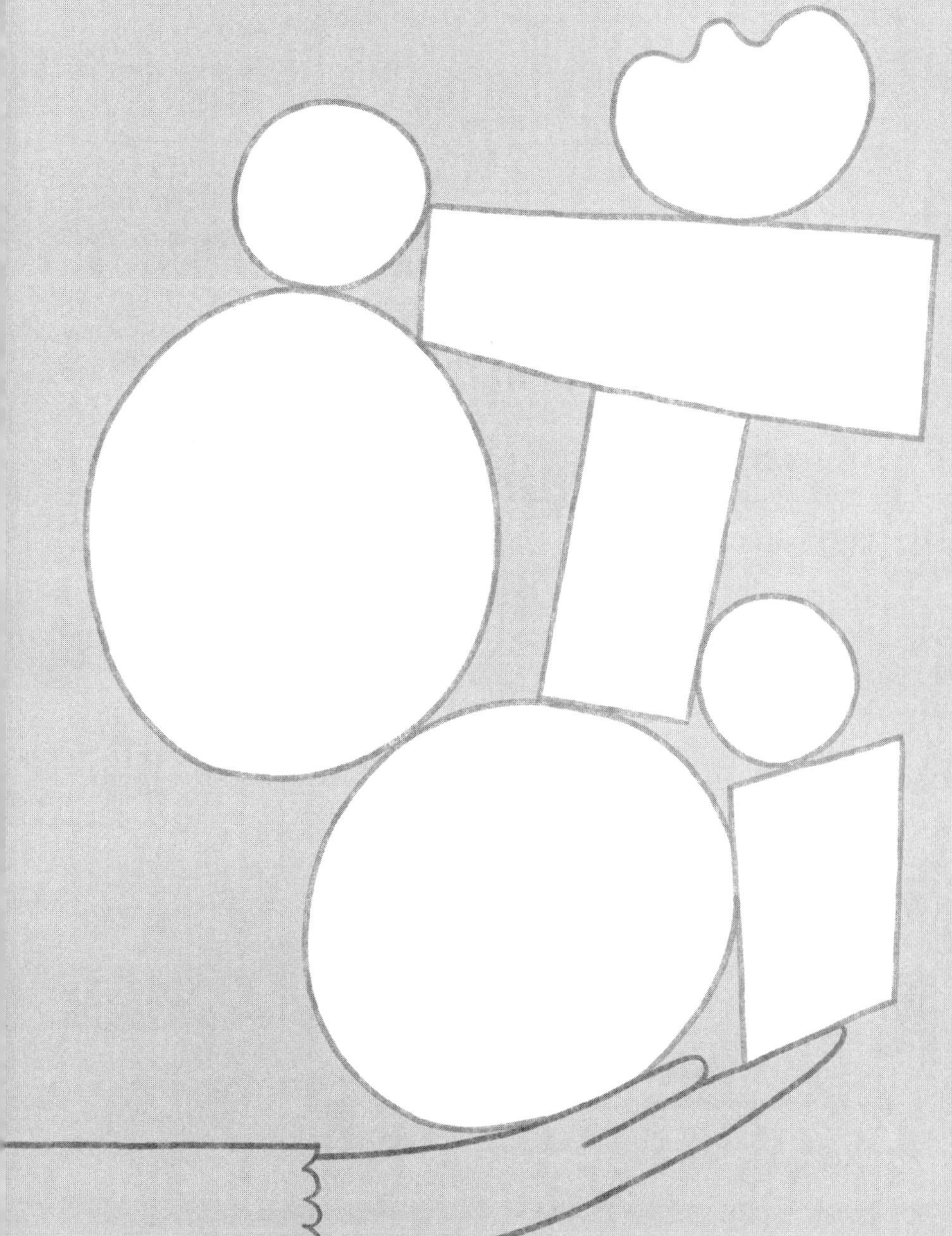

QUALITY TIME

PHYSICAL TOUCH

WORDS OF AFFIRMATION

ACTS OF SERVICE

GIFTS

"The 5 Love Languages"
as coined by Gary Chapman

we can all enjoy a whole mix of
caring gestures, but maybe we notice
one or two of these love languages
feel more potent & central to us.

do you crave to hear words of love or is
care for you best expressed with touch?
maybe time together, without anywhere
to be, is what really fills your cup.

when we understand the gestures that
feel most meaningful to us, we can share
that insight with anyone who wants
to learn how to love us better & can be
mindful of their preferences too.

if a special someone wants to show me love
or appreciation, what do i hope they say?
what are the words i crave to hear?

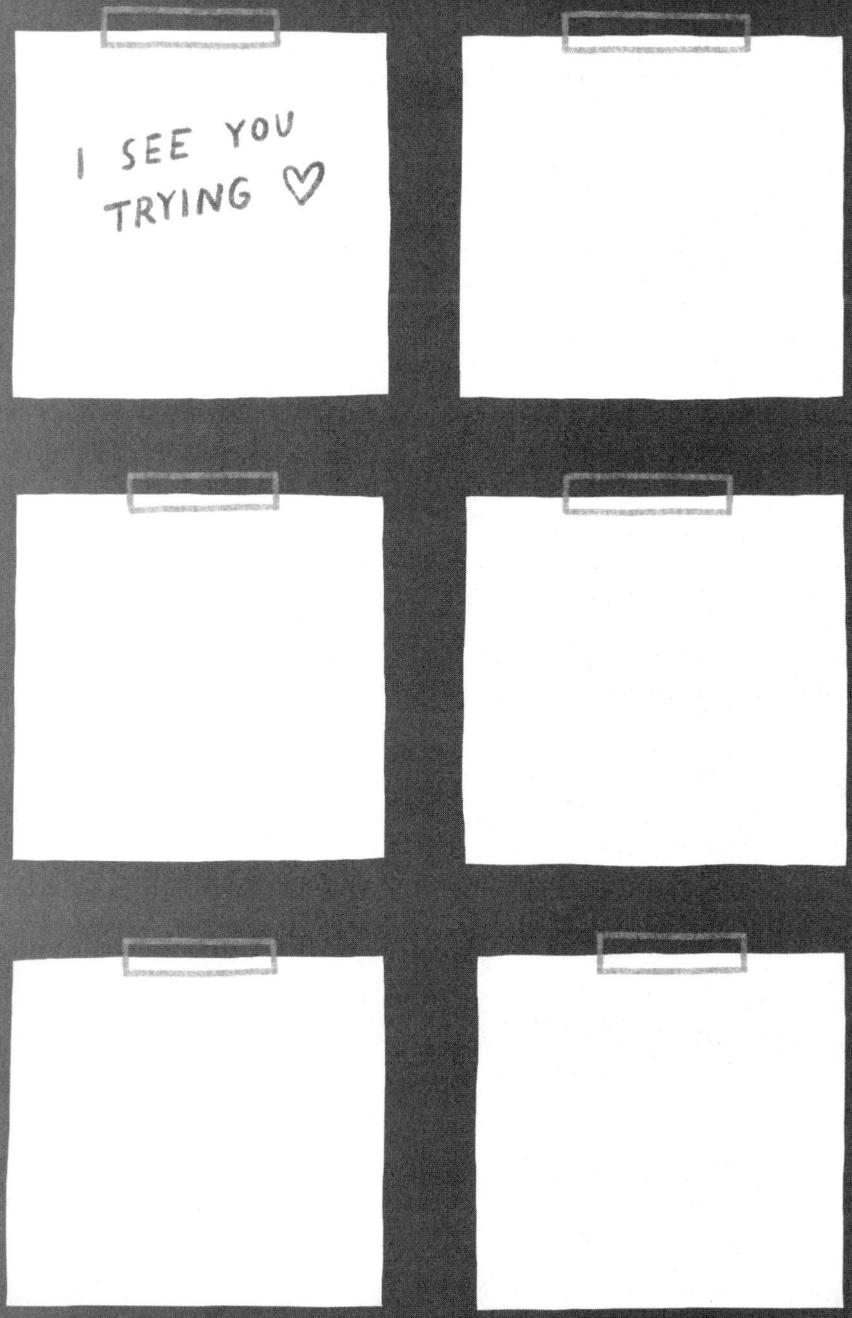

I SEE YOU
TRYING ♡

if a special someone wants to show me love
or appreciation, what could they do for me?
what items on my to-do list, or in my day,
would i love for someone to take care of?

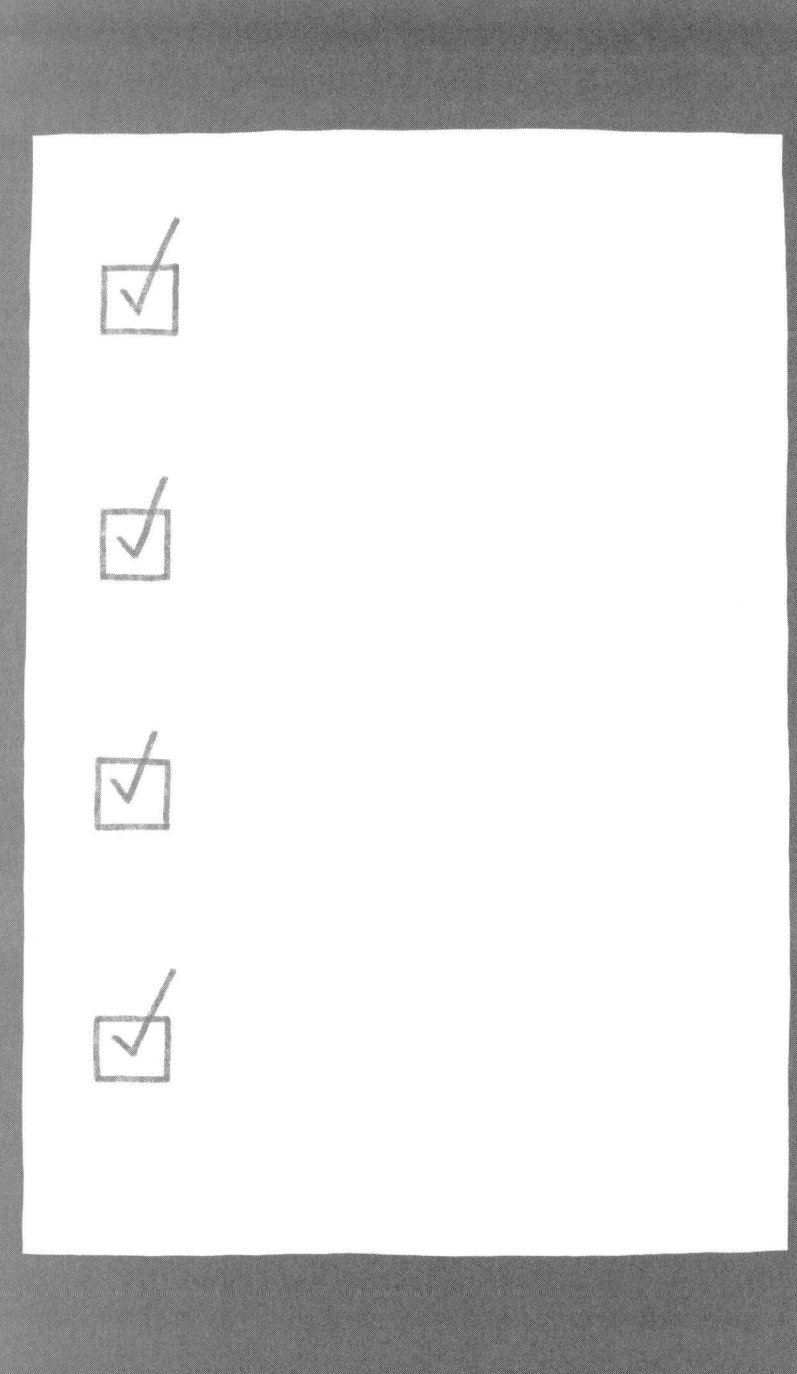

if a special someone wants to show me love
or appreciation, what do i hope they bring?
what are some "just because" gifts to
really warm my heart?

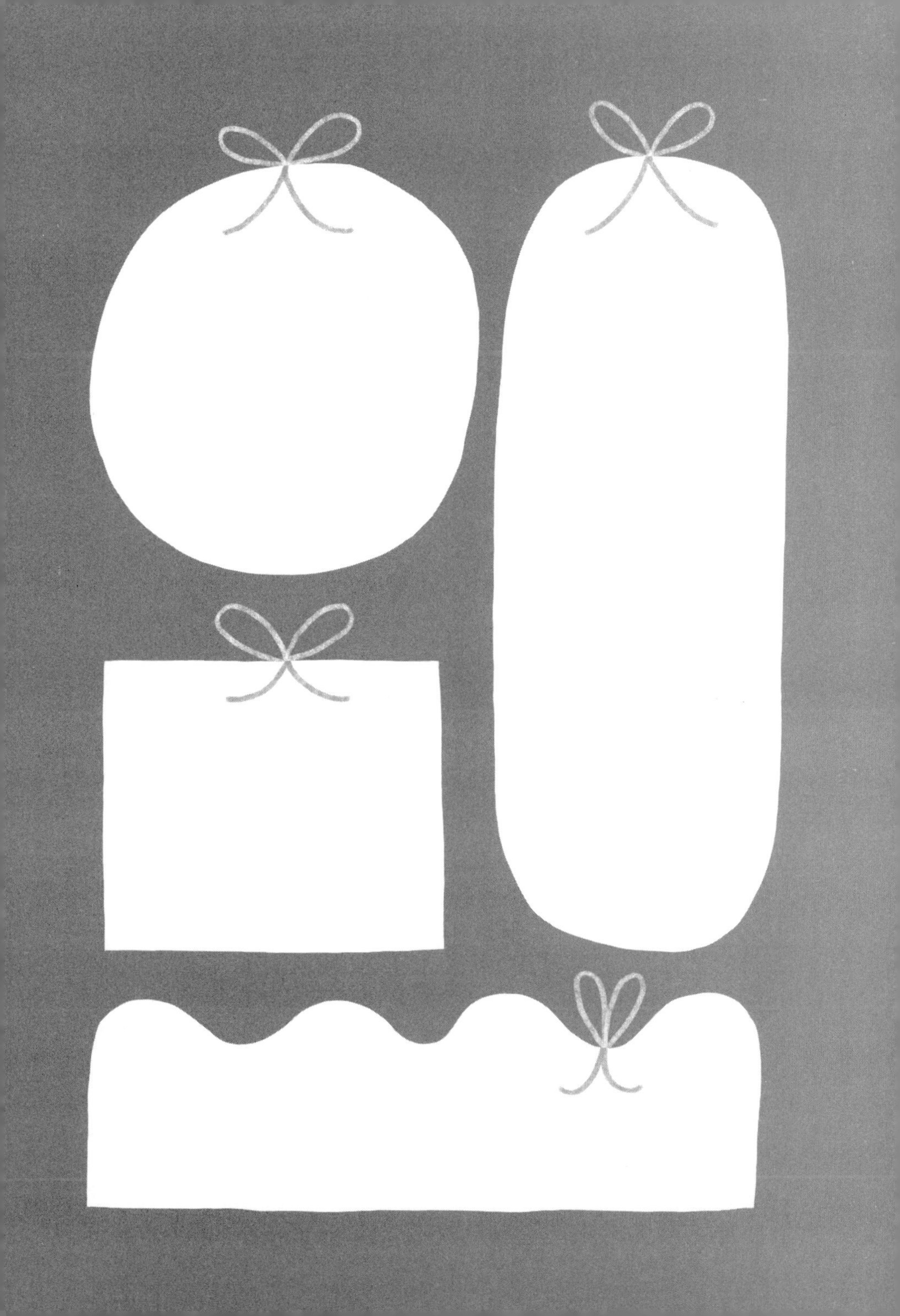

if a special someone wants to show me love
or appreciation, what kind of touch feels
sweet, comforting or delicious in my body?
what are the tactile affections i crave?

(always with ongoing consent, of course!)

30

NIGHT

AFTERNOON

MORNING

if a special someone wants to show me love or appreciation, what kind of date do i hope they plan? what, for me, does quality time together really mean?

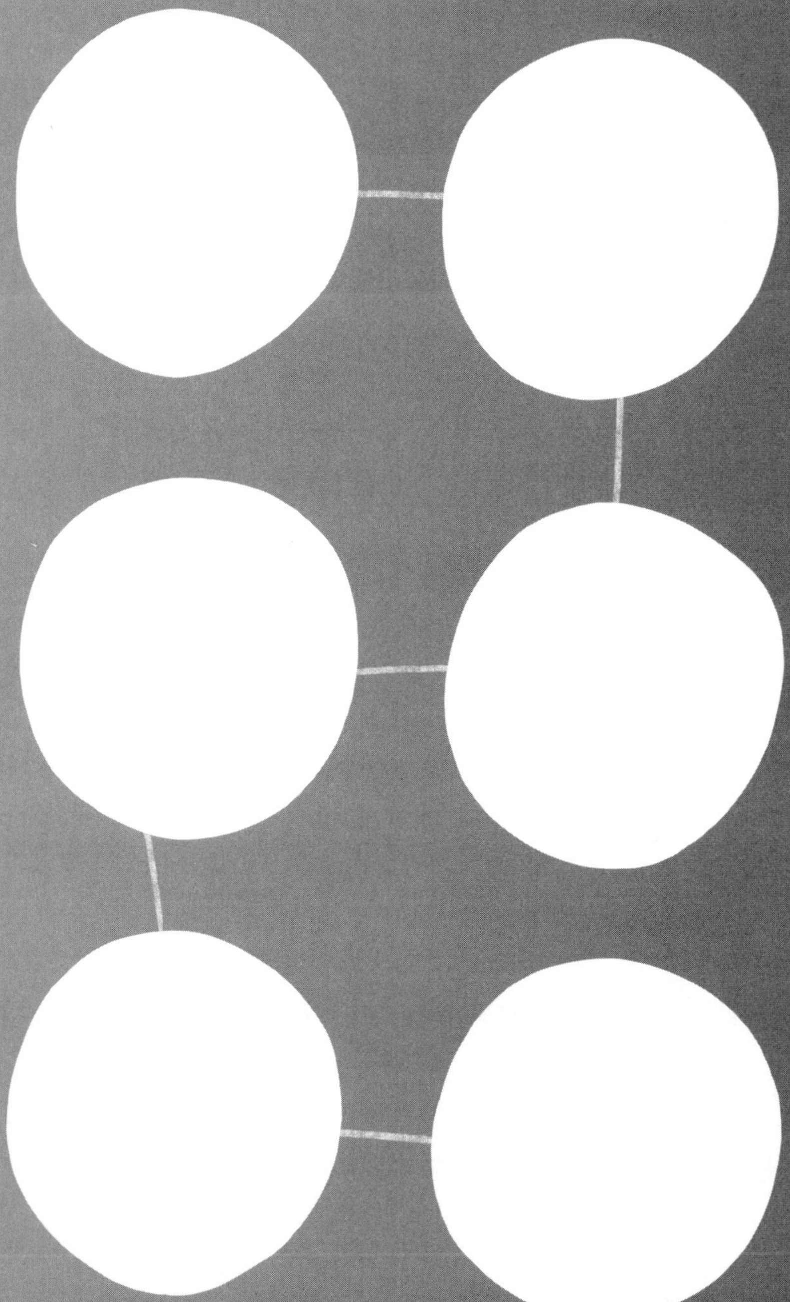

when i daydream five
or ten years ahead,
what are the different
life paths i can maybe
see myself traveling on?
what feelings do they
each spark for me?

35

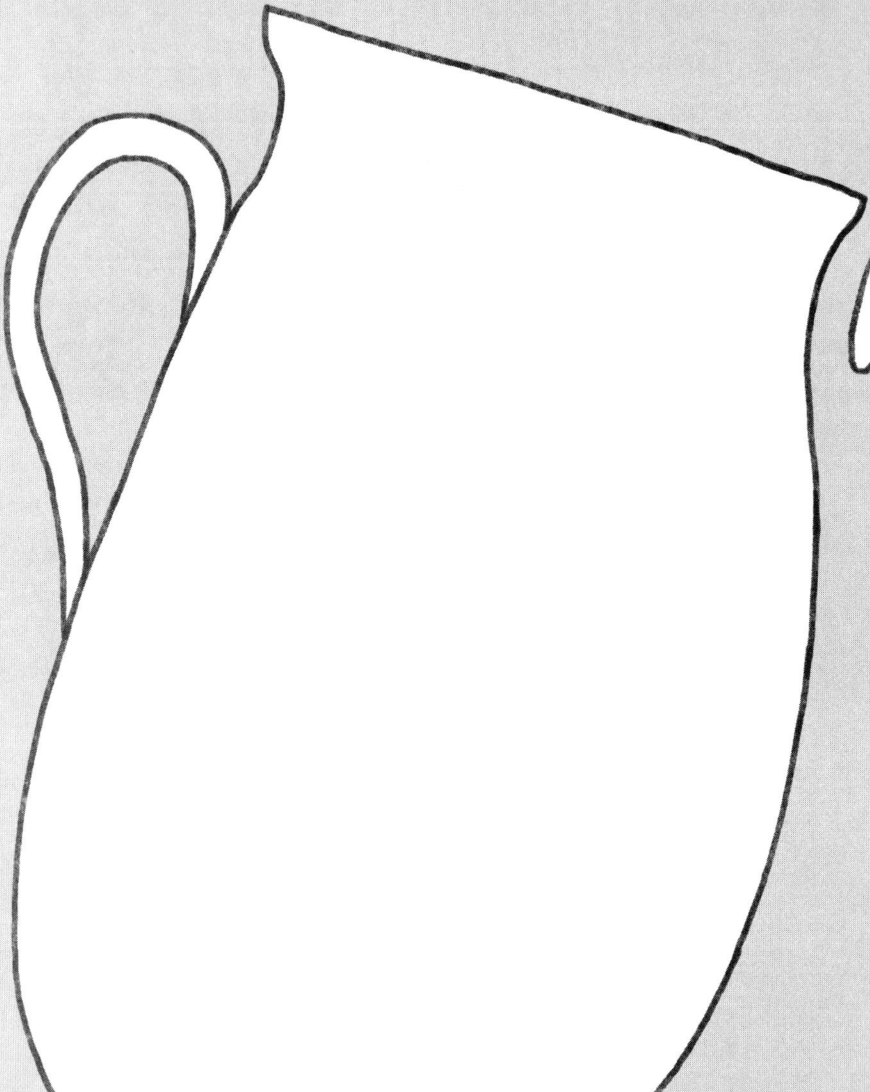

the love i'm aching to give

the love i'm ready to receive

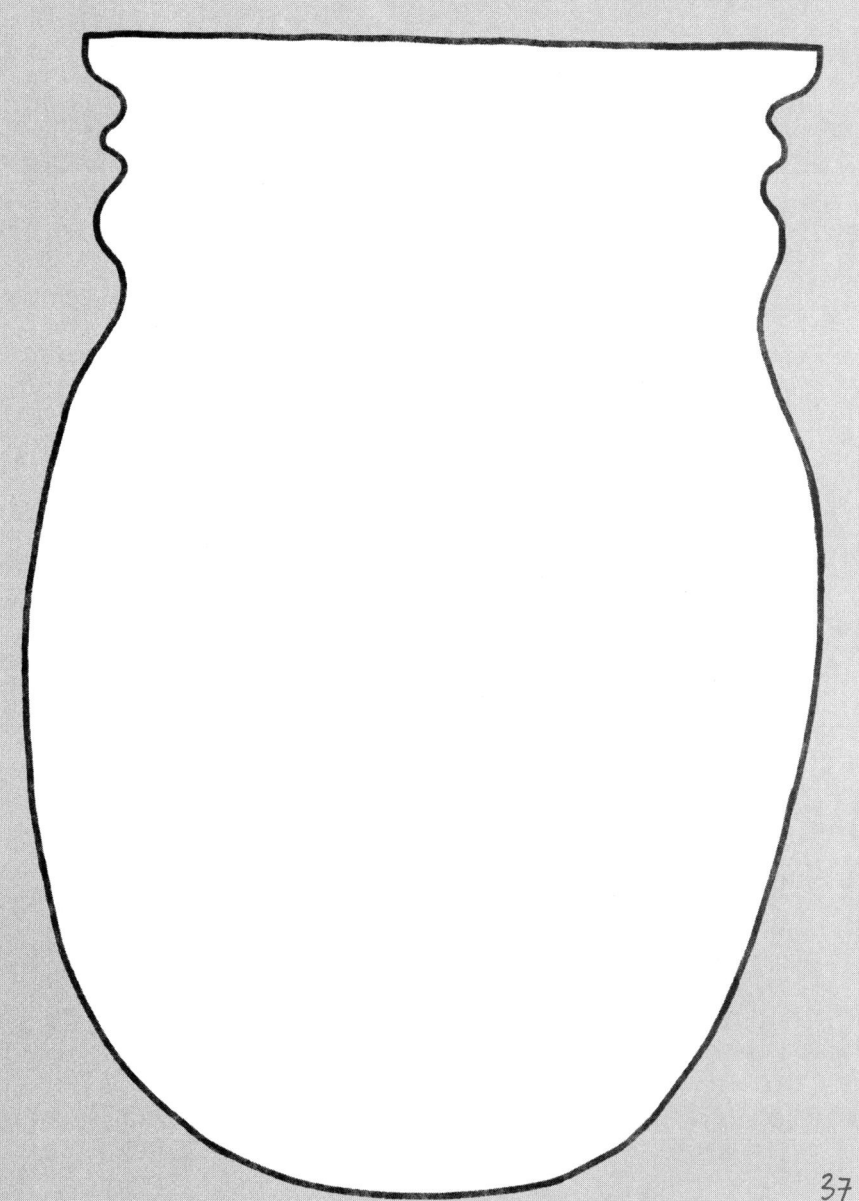

37

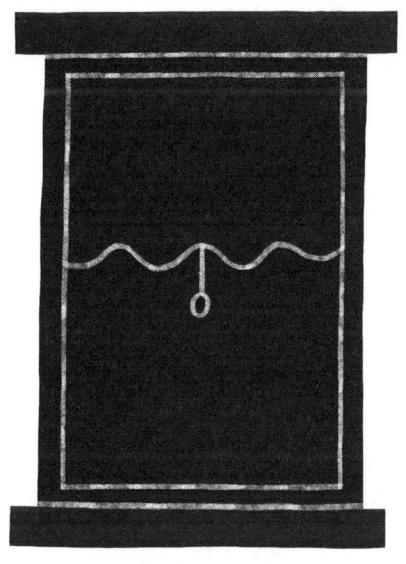

REFLECTIONS

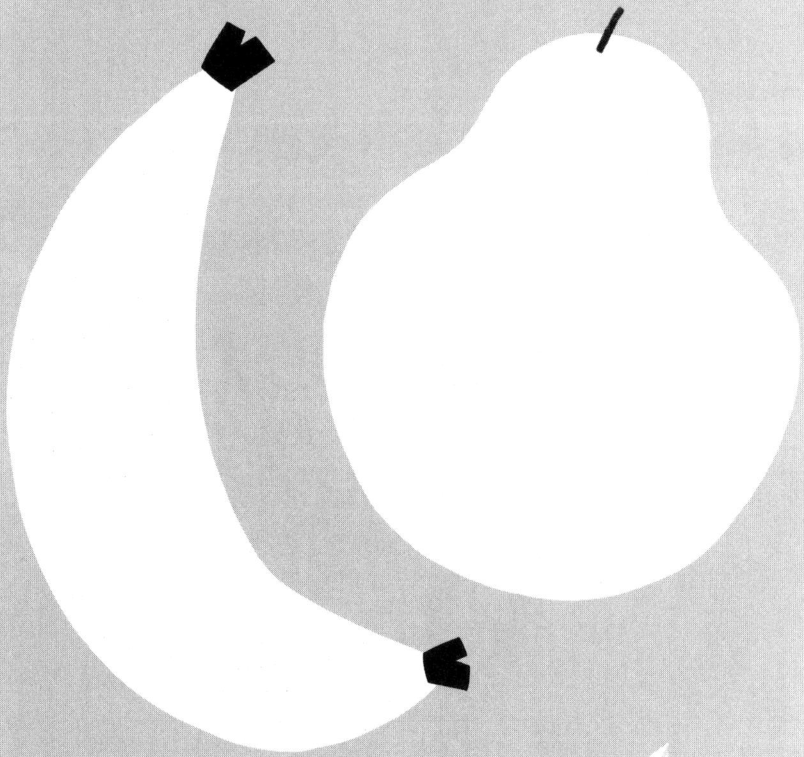

what big hopes or
life goals am i most
determined or excited
to reach for lately?

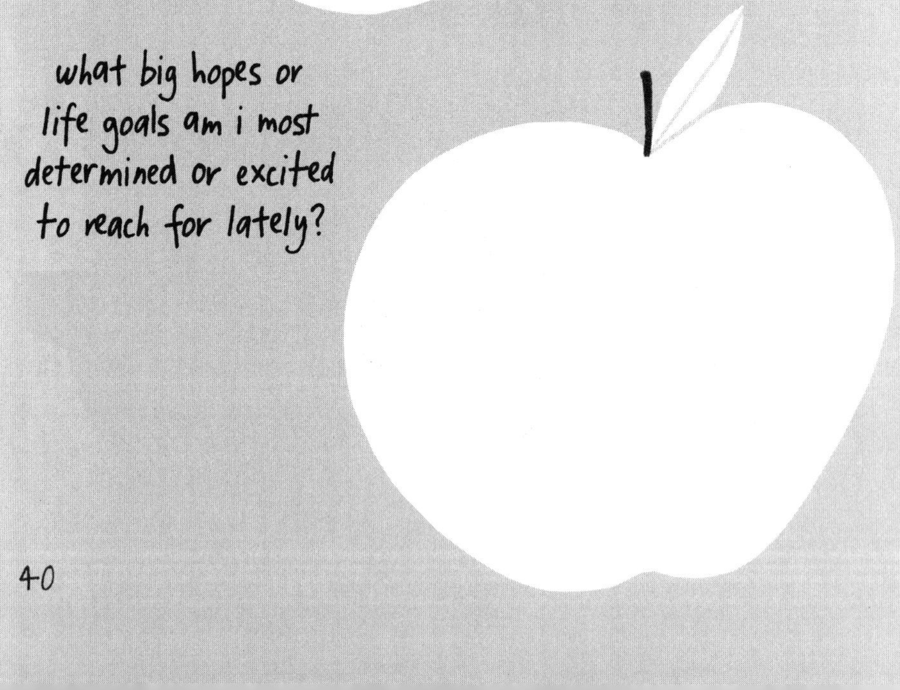

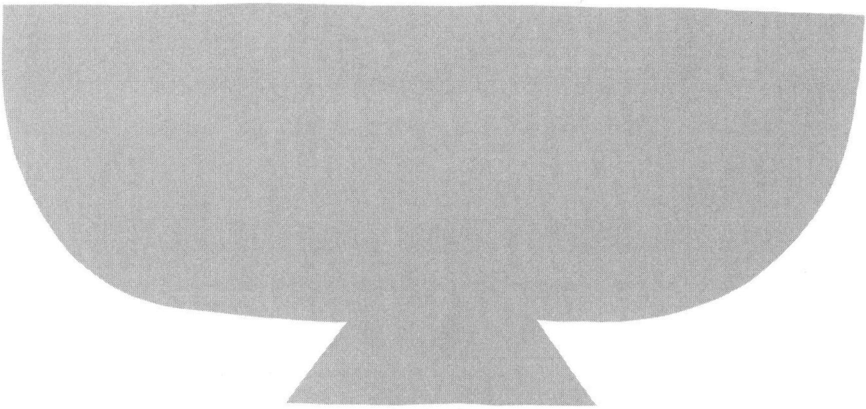

when i look around my life as it is today,
what do i feel thankful for?

growing up, what did the adults in my life
(or movies & tv) teach me about love?

what relationship lessons, sweet or cynical,
have stuck with me in some way?

43

as one half of a loving relationship,
where do i know i'd blossom? in what ways
do i love to contribute & show care?

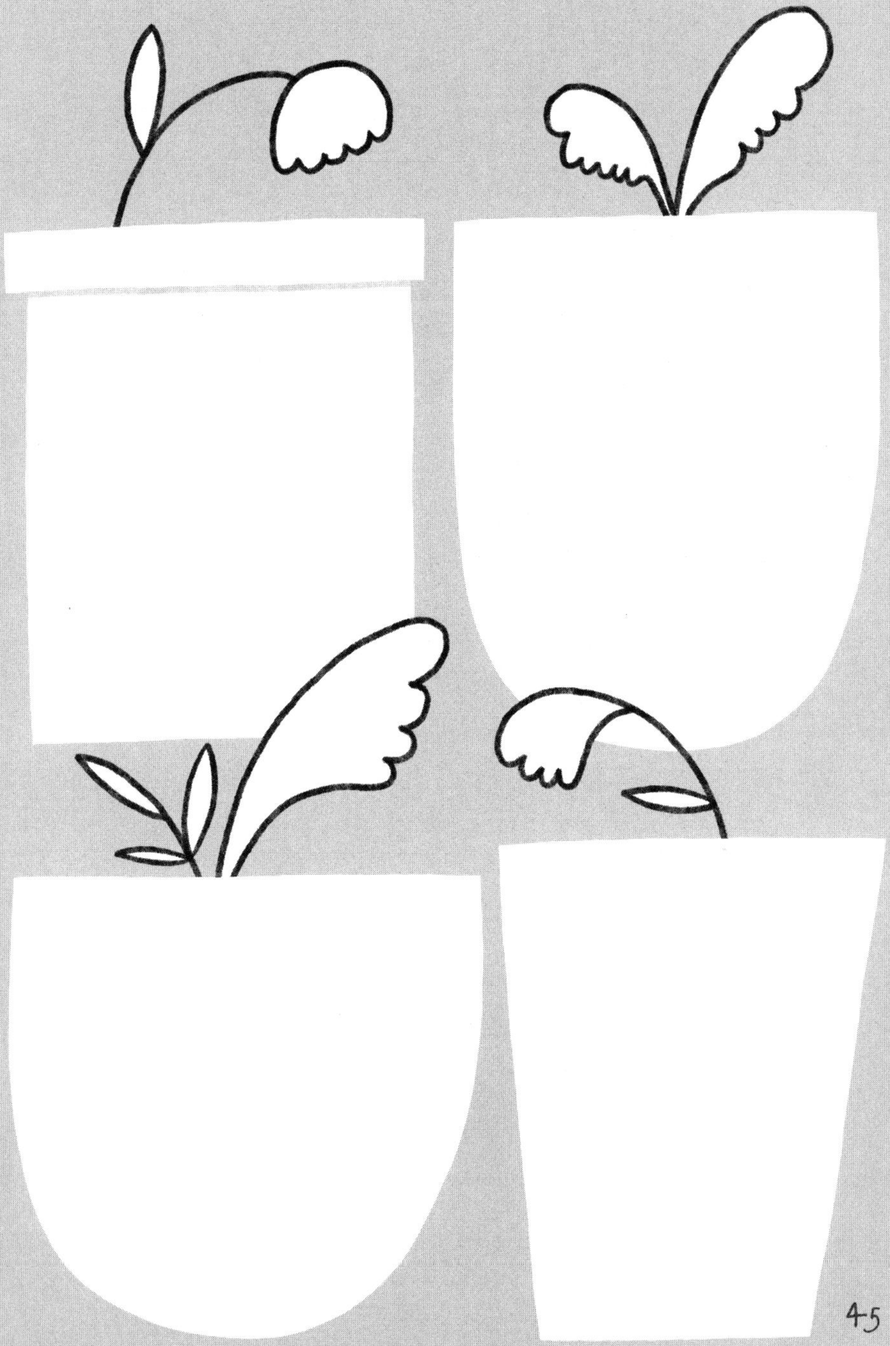

# A QUICK TOUR OF MY DATING HISTORY

a memorable conversation

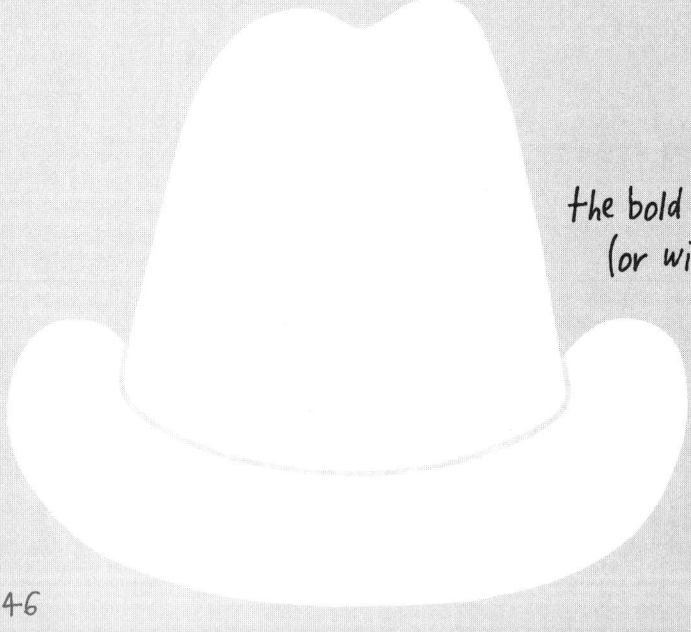

the bold move i made (or wish i had!)

a sweet gesture
i won't forget

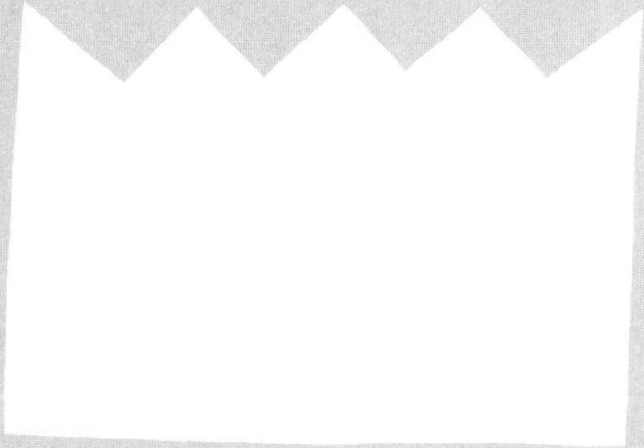

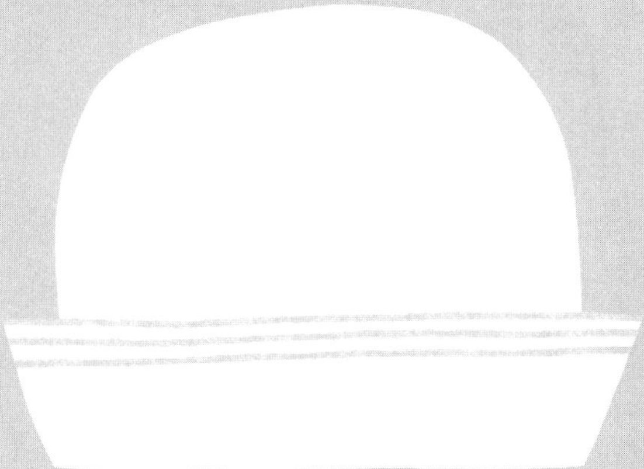

rough seas i had
to navigate my
way out of

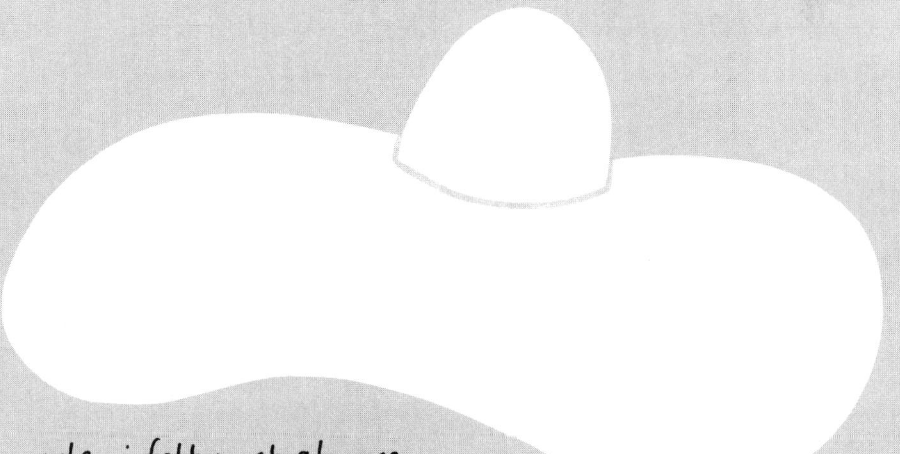

when i felt most at ease

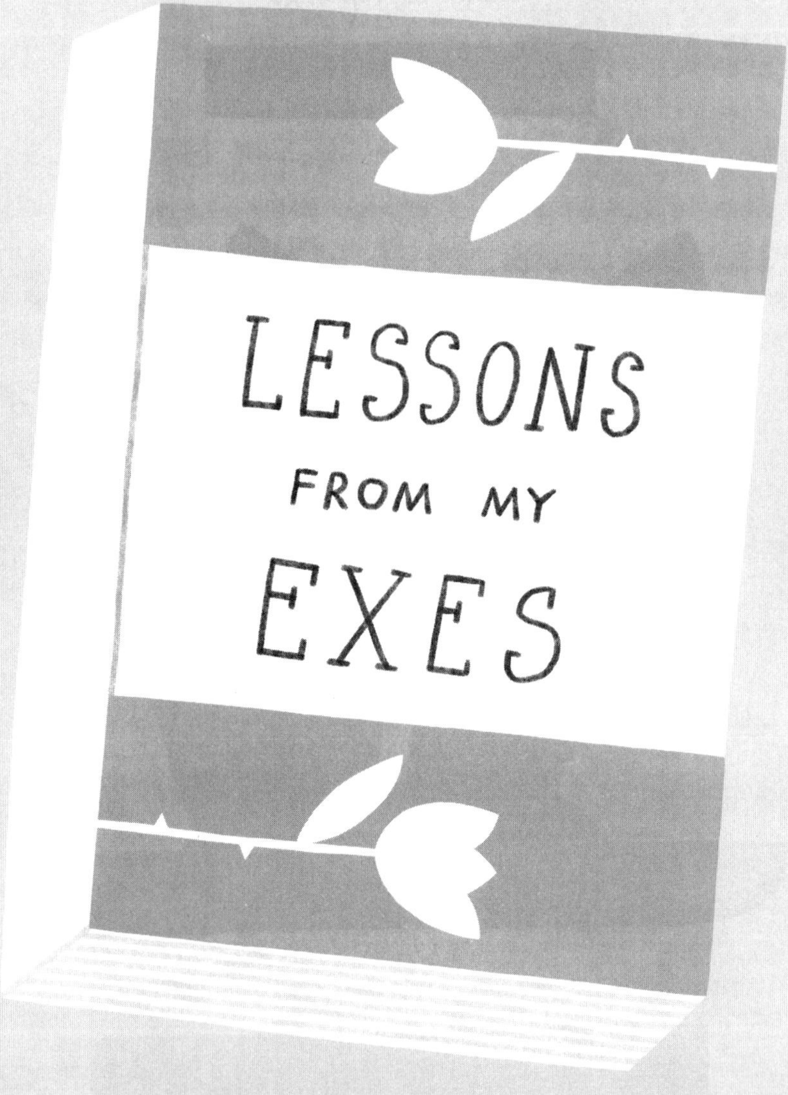
LESSONS
FROM MY
EXES

(or anyone i've been romantically entangled with in some way)

# CHAPTER I

# CHAPTER II

# CHAPTER III

# CHAPTER IV

what are some things that feel really
fun or attractive to me when i first meet
someone but i know probably aren't a good
fit for me in the long run?

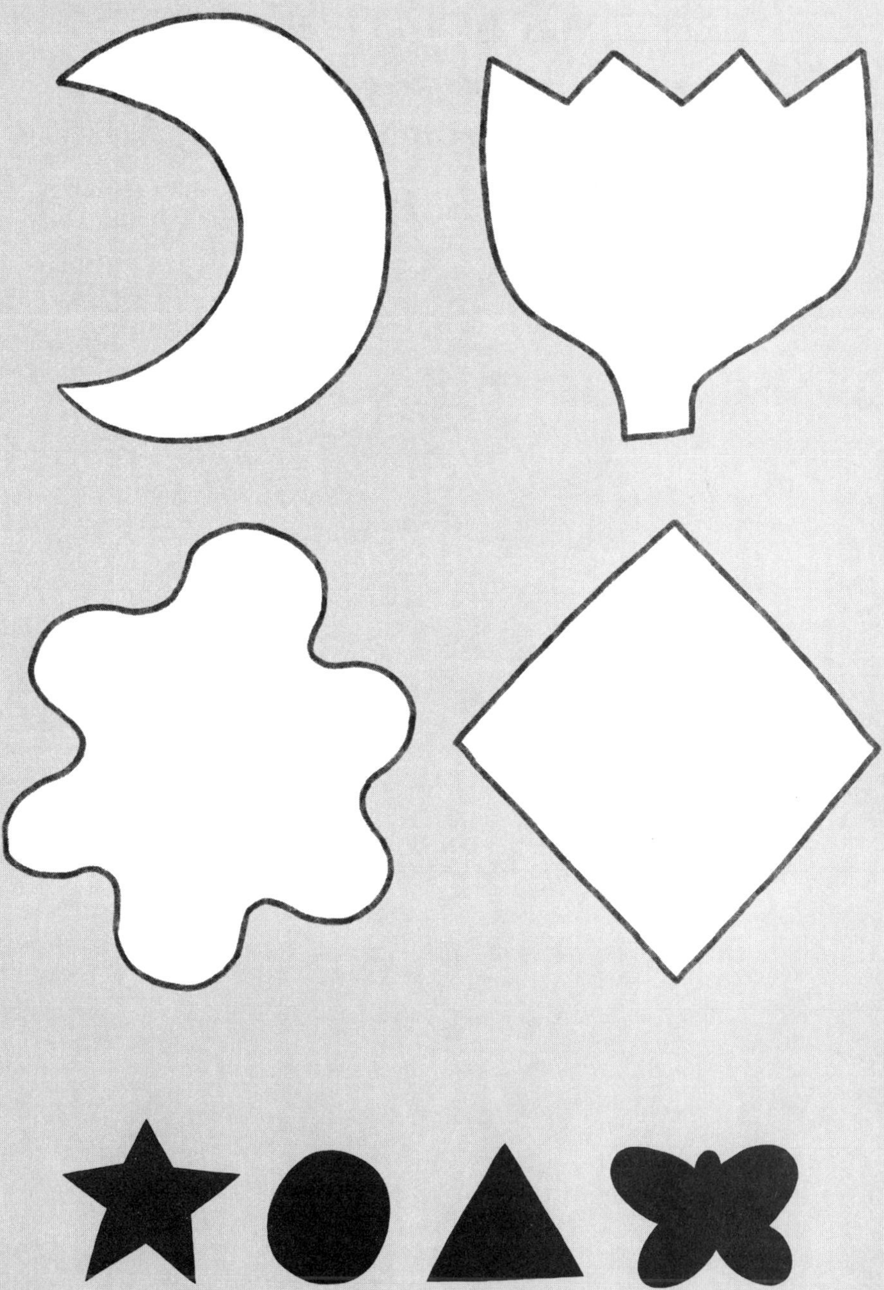

what qualities do i tend to think will make me more lovable or desirable, even if they're not really me?

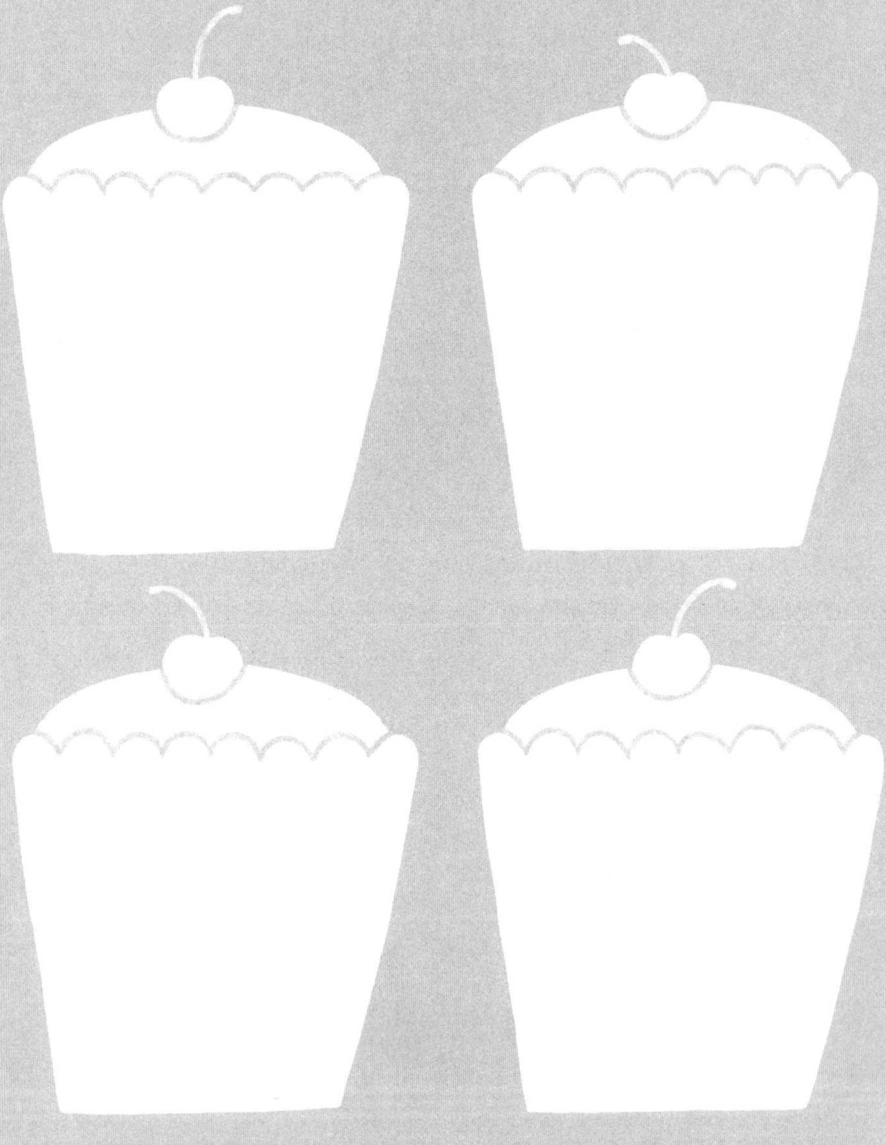

how do i know i'm feeling safe & comfortable
to be my whole, authentic self with someone?
what are the signs i can look for?

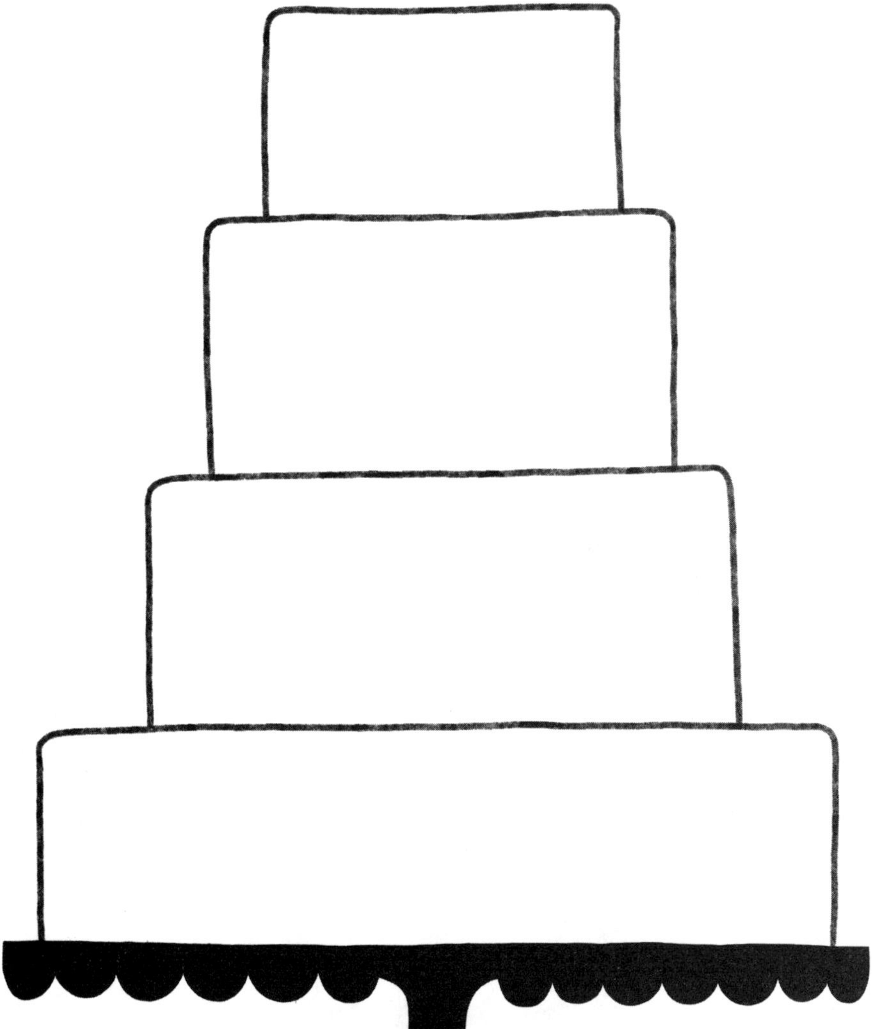

three ways i try to protect
my heart & keep it safe
from harm

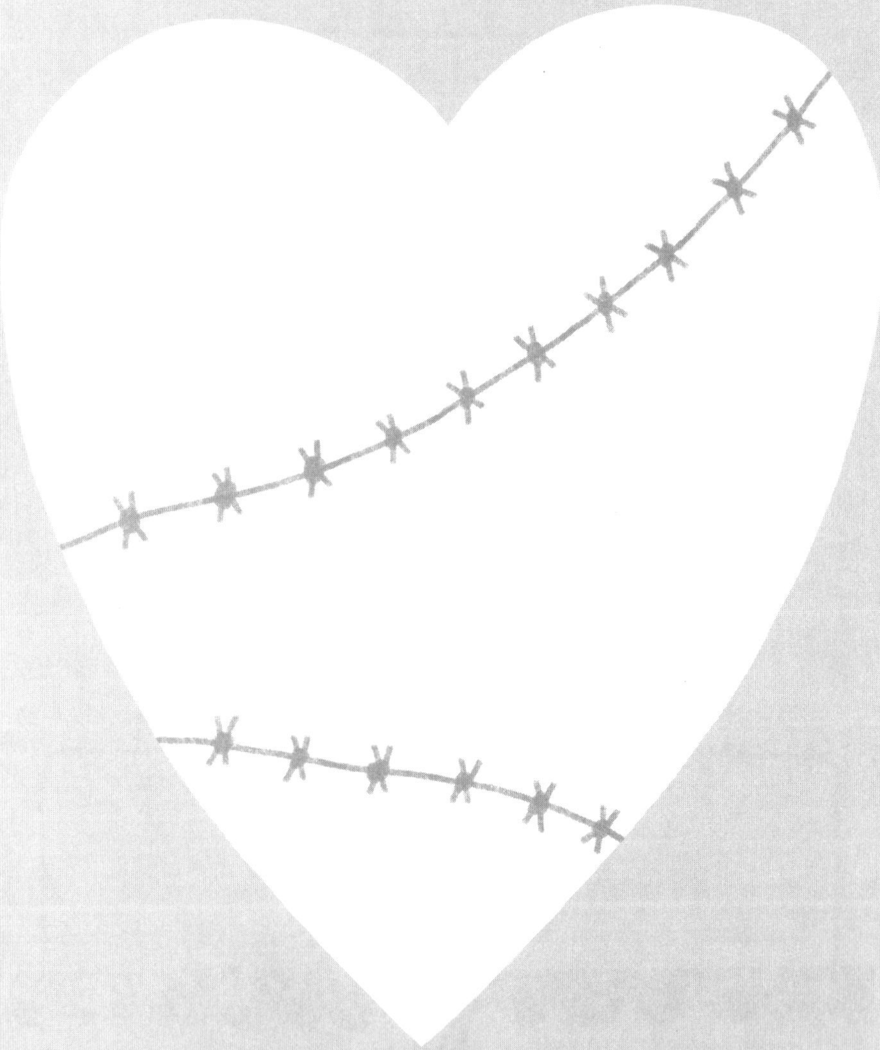

if i did wear my
heart on my sleeve,
what might it say?

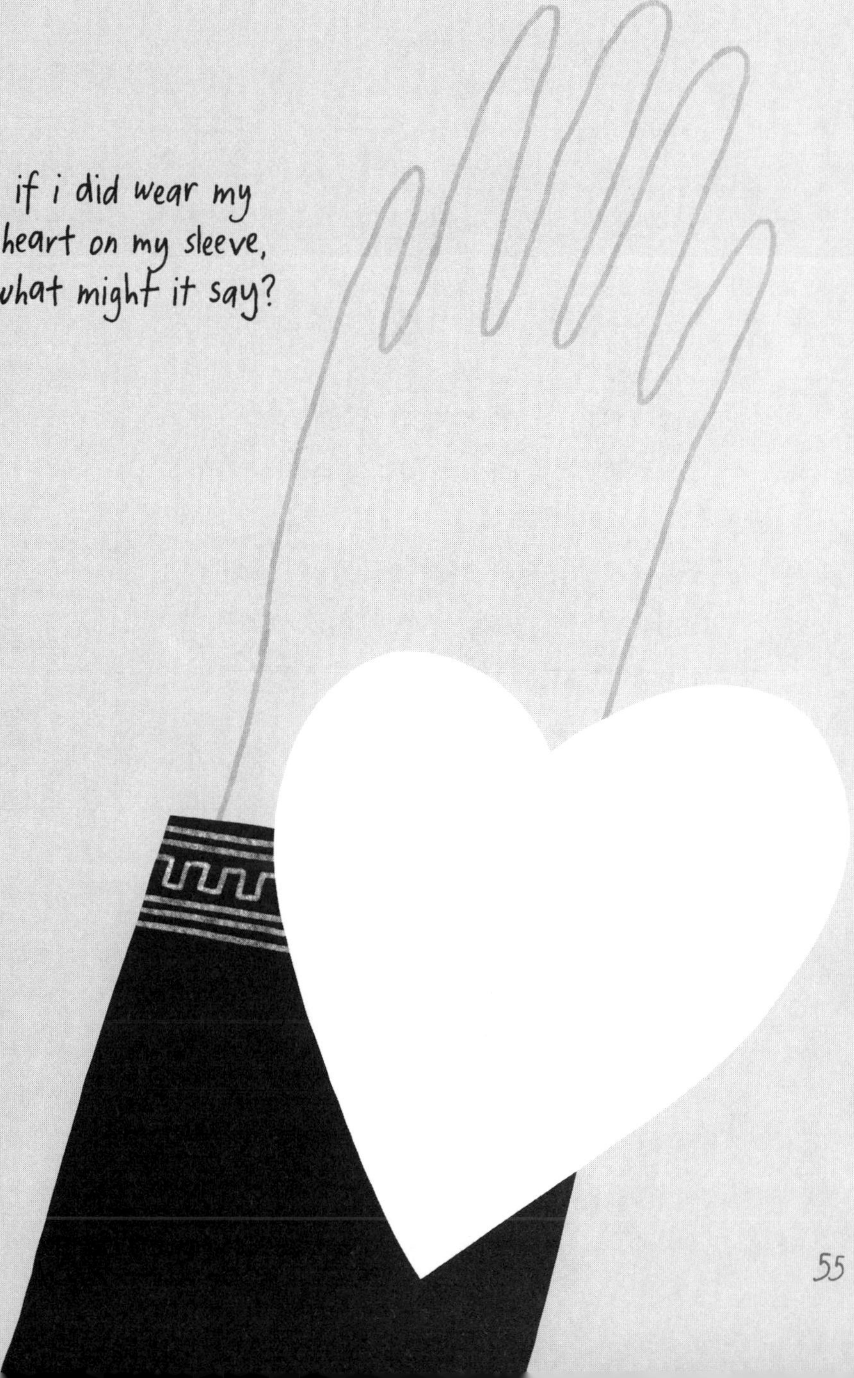

what kind of person would do
the best job of loving me?

what have i learned (or always known)
are my three most important needs
I would want them to care for?

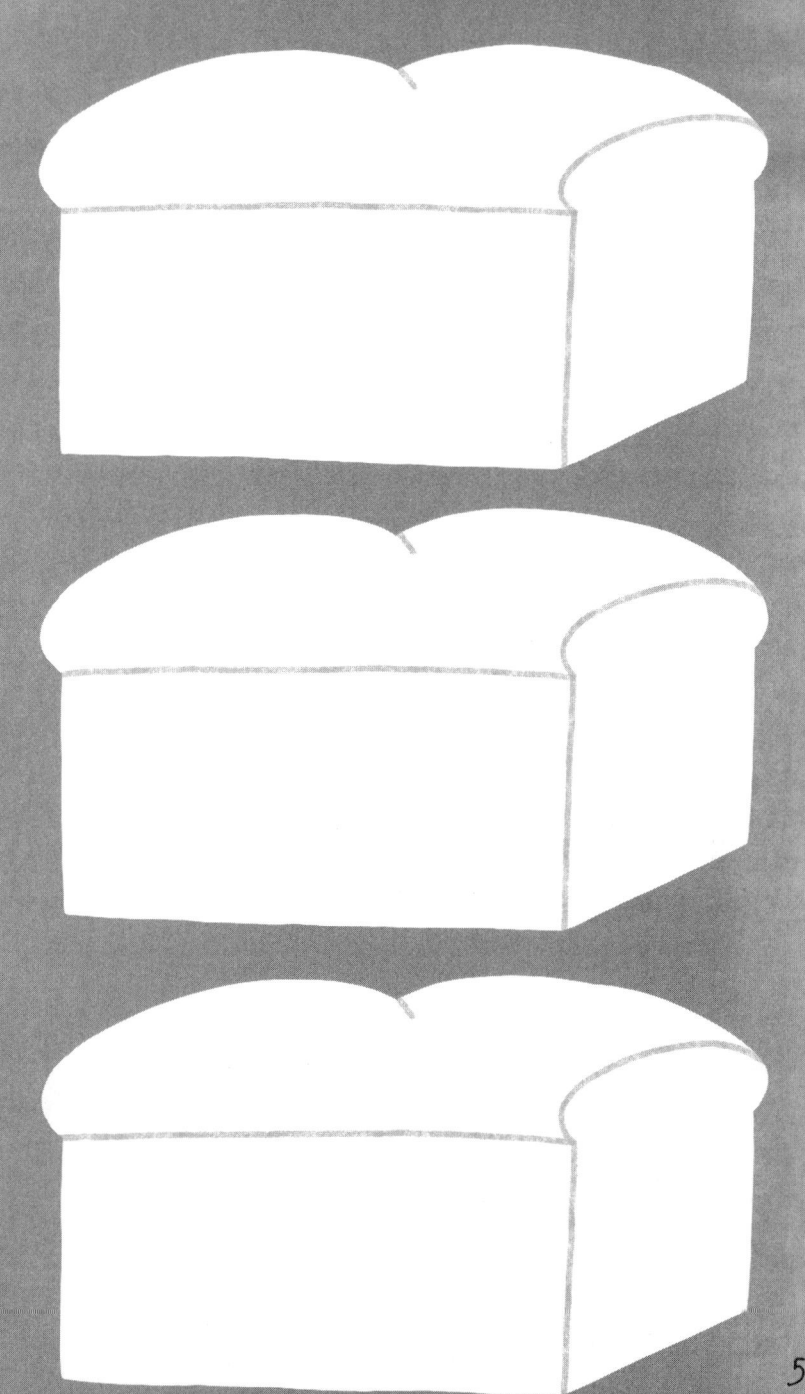

57

what would it look like for someone
to show care for those needs?
what could they do?

if someone was offering me only crumbs,
what might that look like?

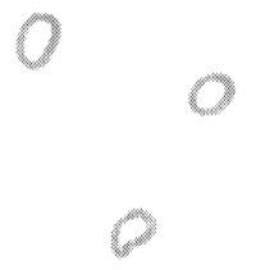

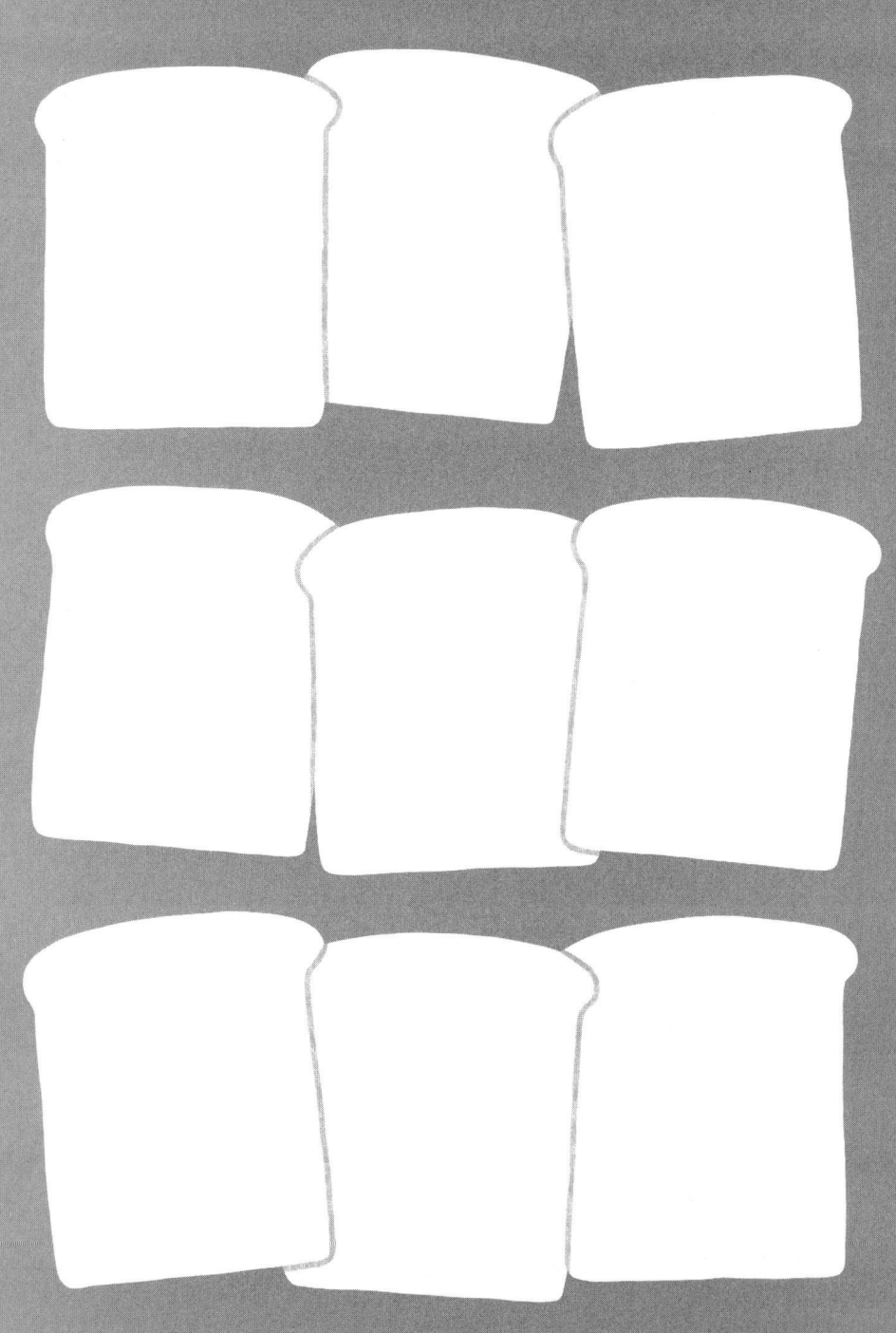

moments lately when i've felt a pang of relationship envy, wishing i had that too

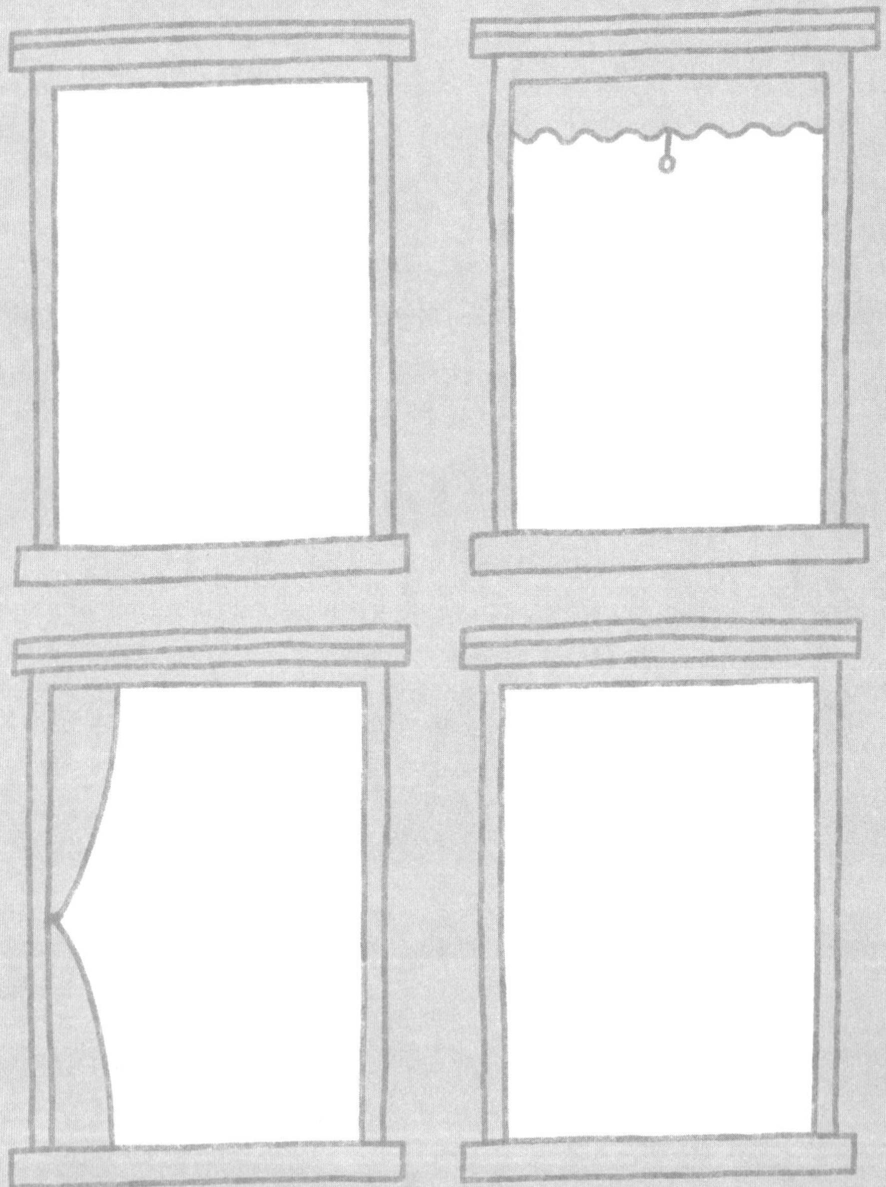

moments i might one day look back on
& miss about this season of my life

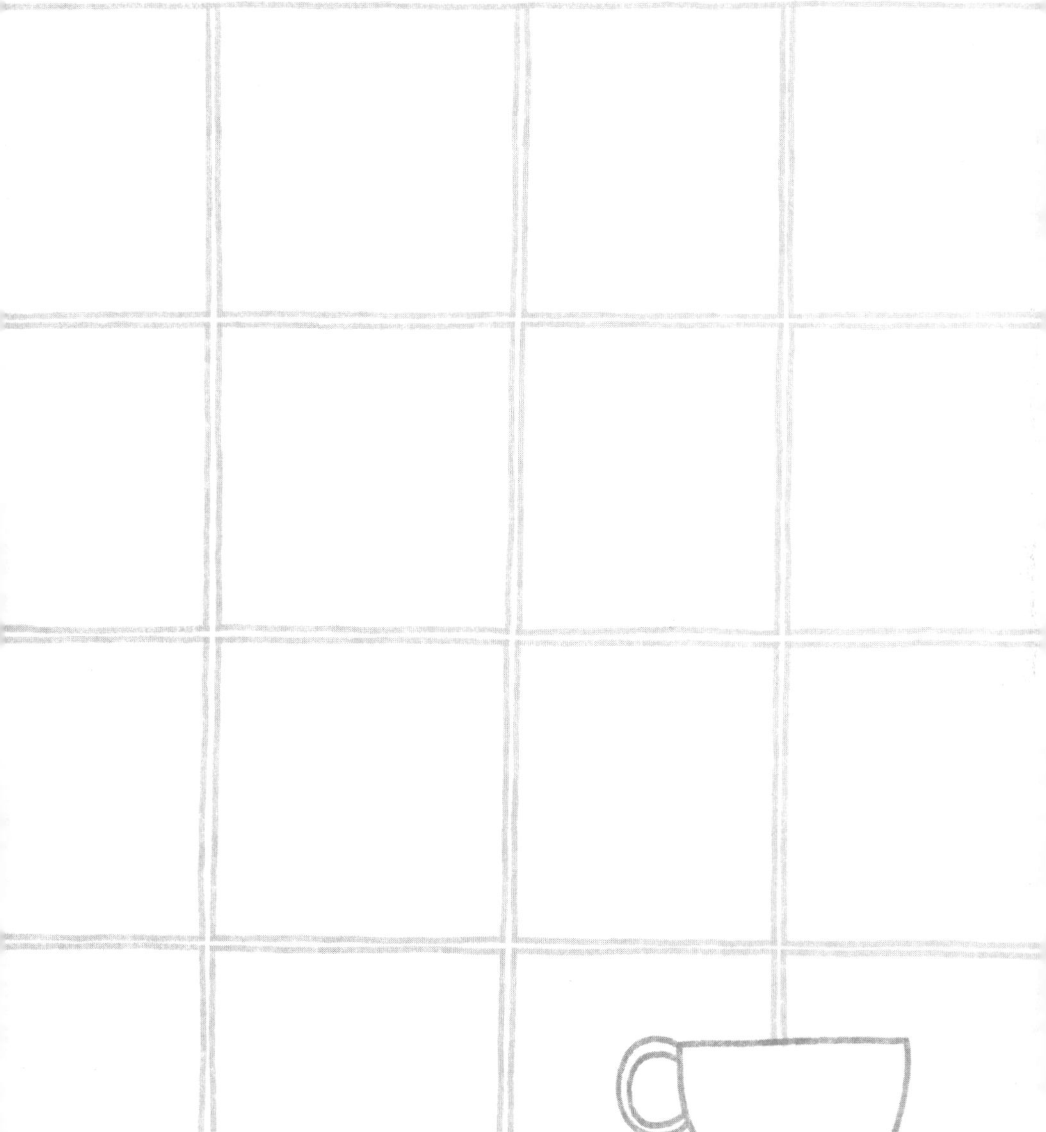

when being on my own feels lonely
& uncomfortable, it's often because

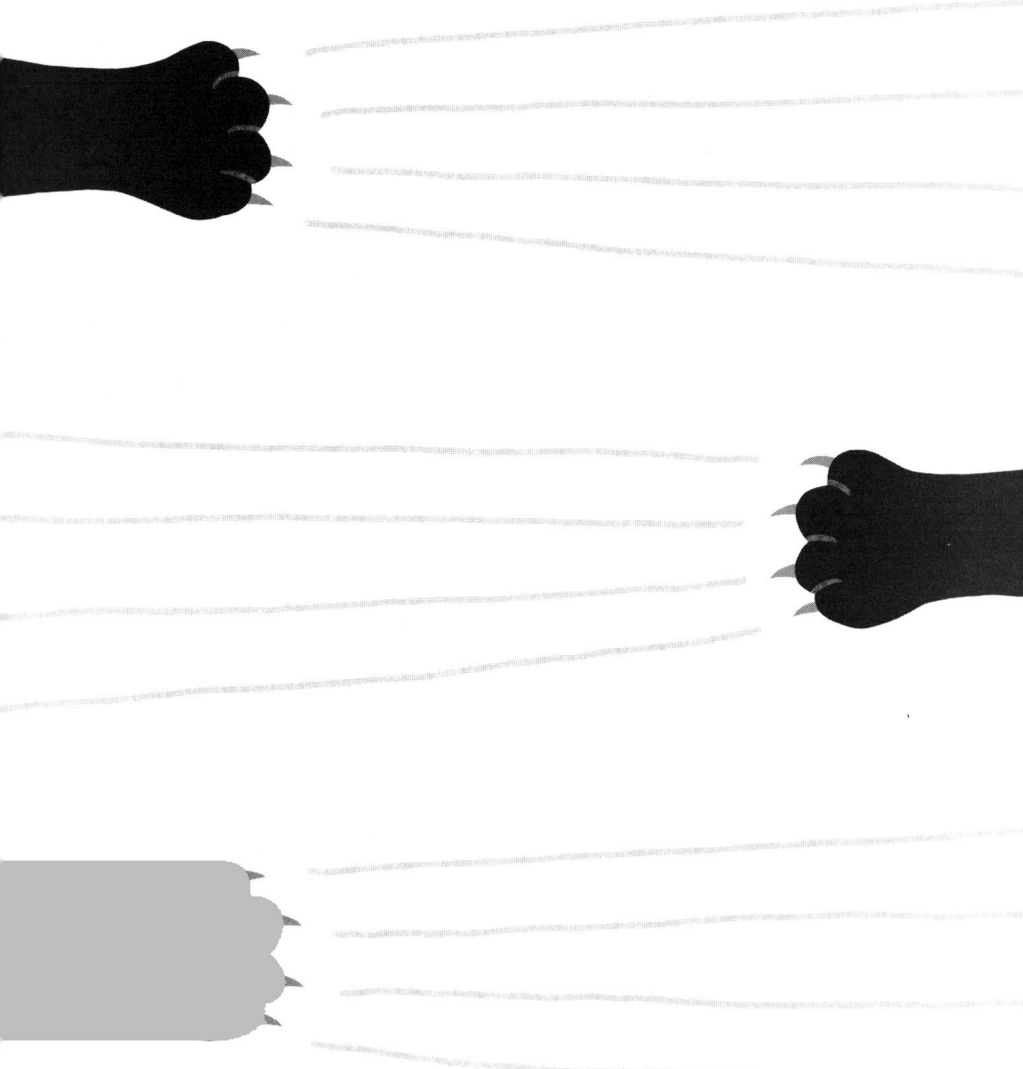

when i'm feeling content & peaceful
in my solitude, it's often because

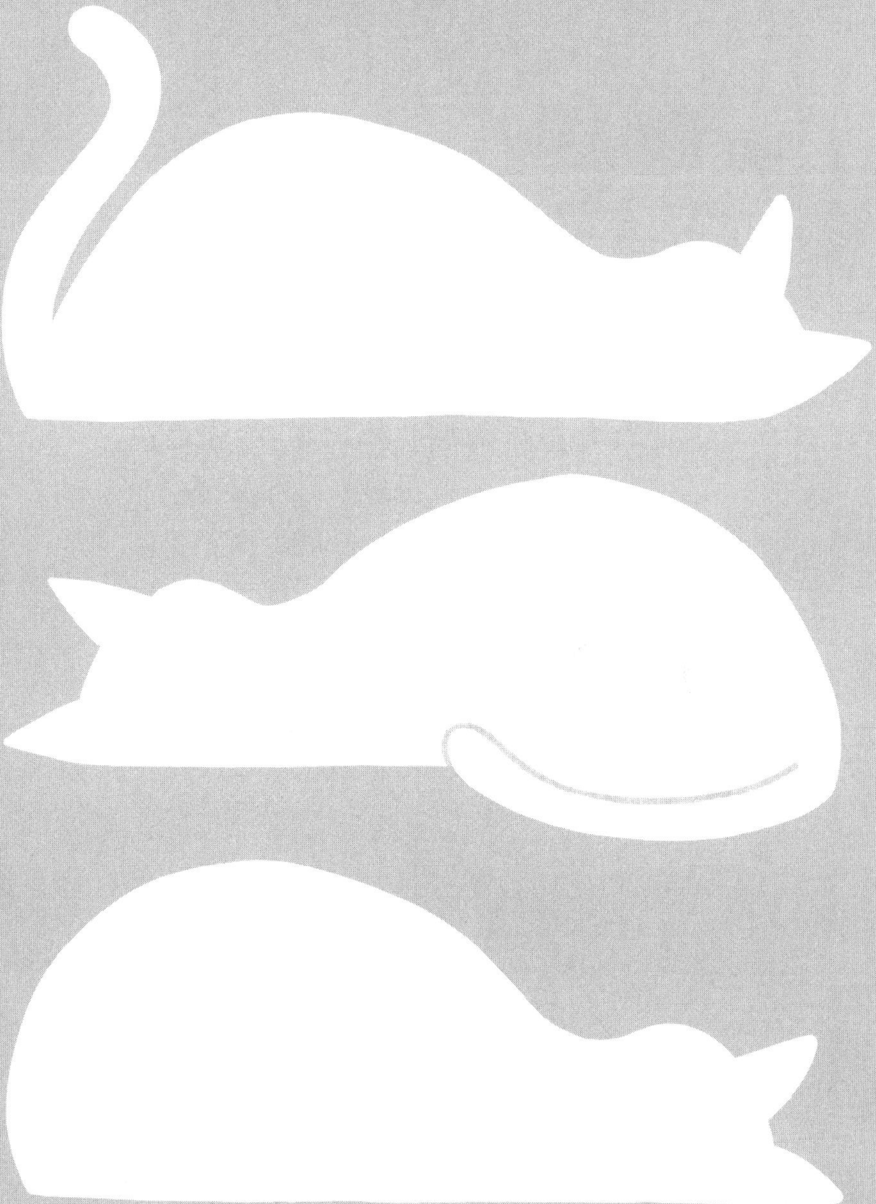

what are the differences in personality
or lifestyle i feel drawn to in a person?
in what ways might a special someone be
a welcome counterbalance in my life?

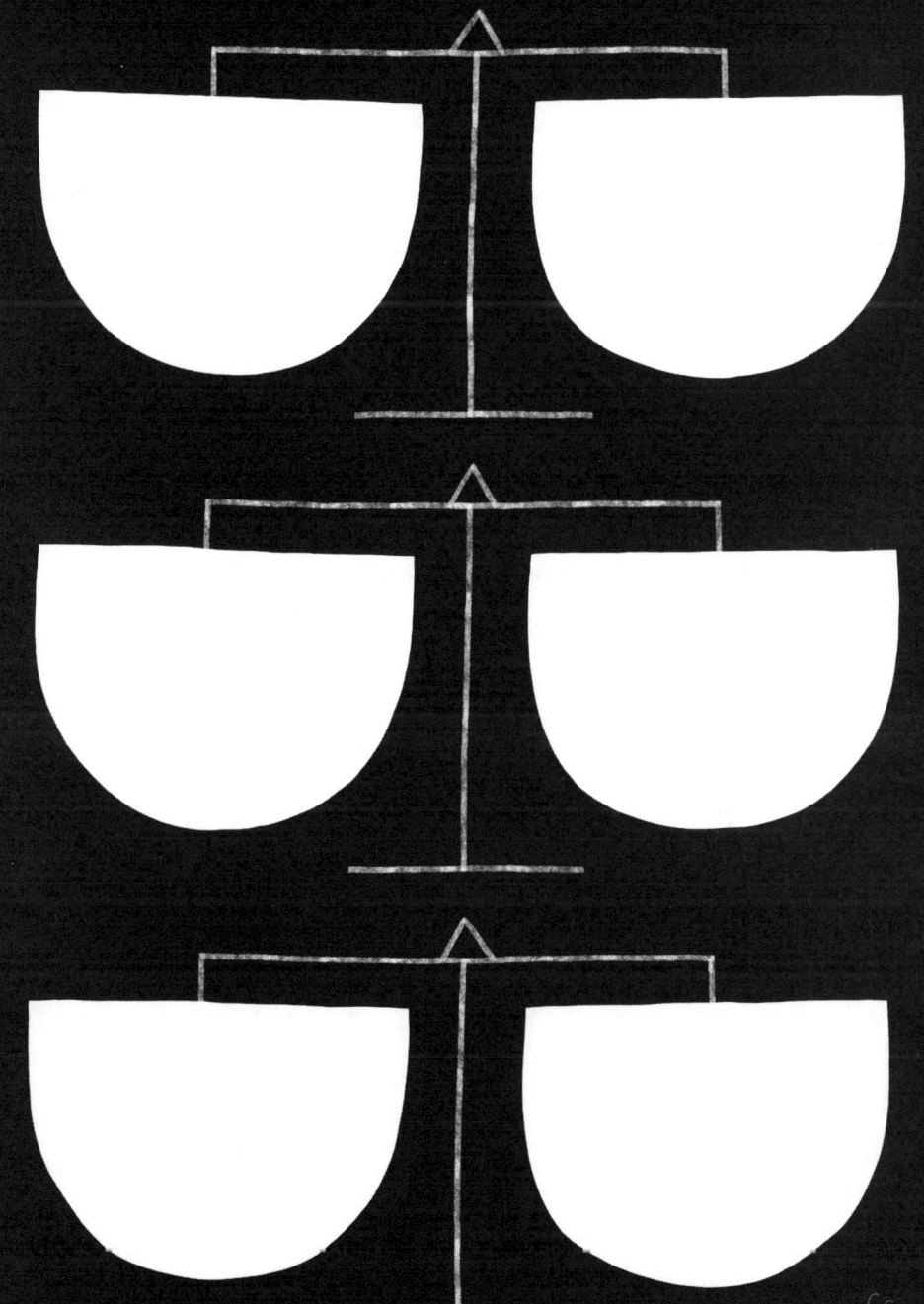

65

what are the similarities in personality
or lifestyle i feel drawn to in a person?
in what ways might our common ground
help us find a home in each other?

i thought the key
to my heart was

but maybe
it's actually

# PEP TALKS

in the garden of my day,
what are the small delights
i'm choosing to tend to?

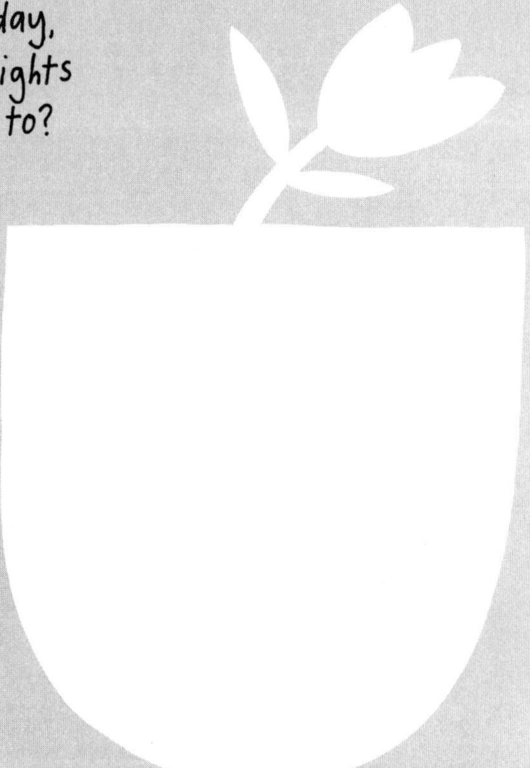

a friendship
in bloom

a splash of
creative flow

the sunshine of
a loved one

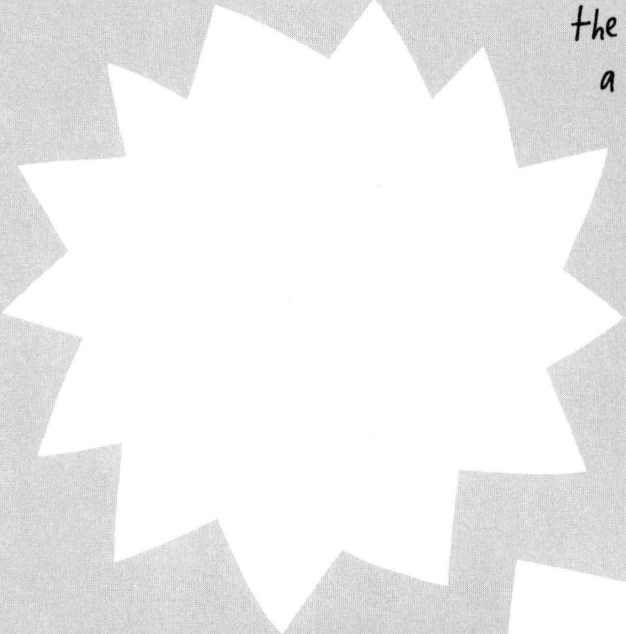

sacred soil to
dig into

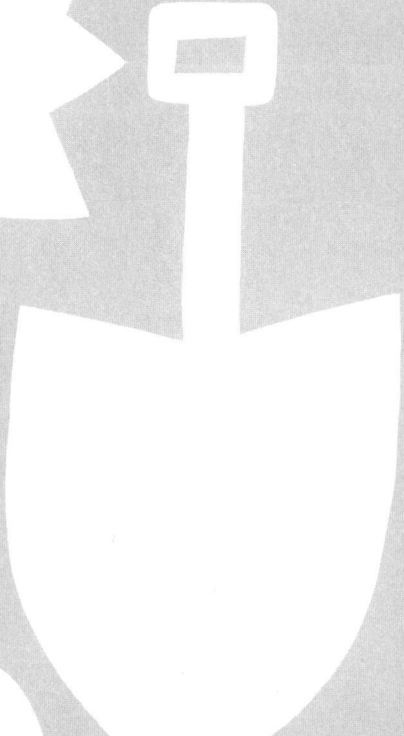

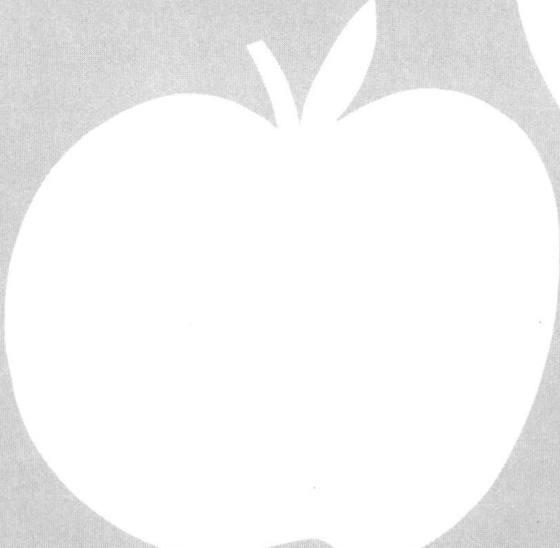

fun that's
ripe to pick

when i'm getting to know someone,
what parts of myself am i usually
eager to share first?

what are the parts of myself
i tend to believe aren't as lovable,
or maybe won't be accepted?

to really feel seen by a special someone,
what hidden parts of myself do i need
to set a place at the table for?

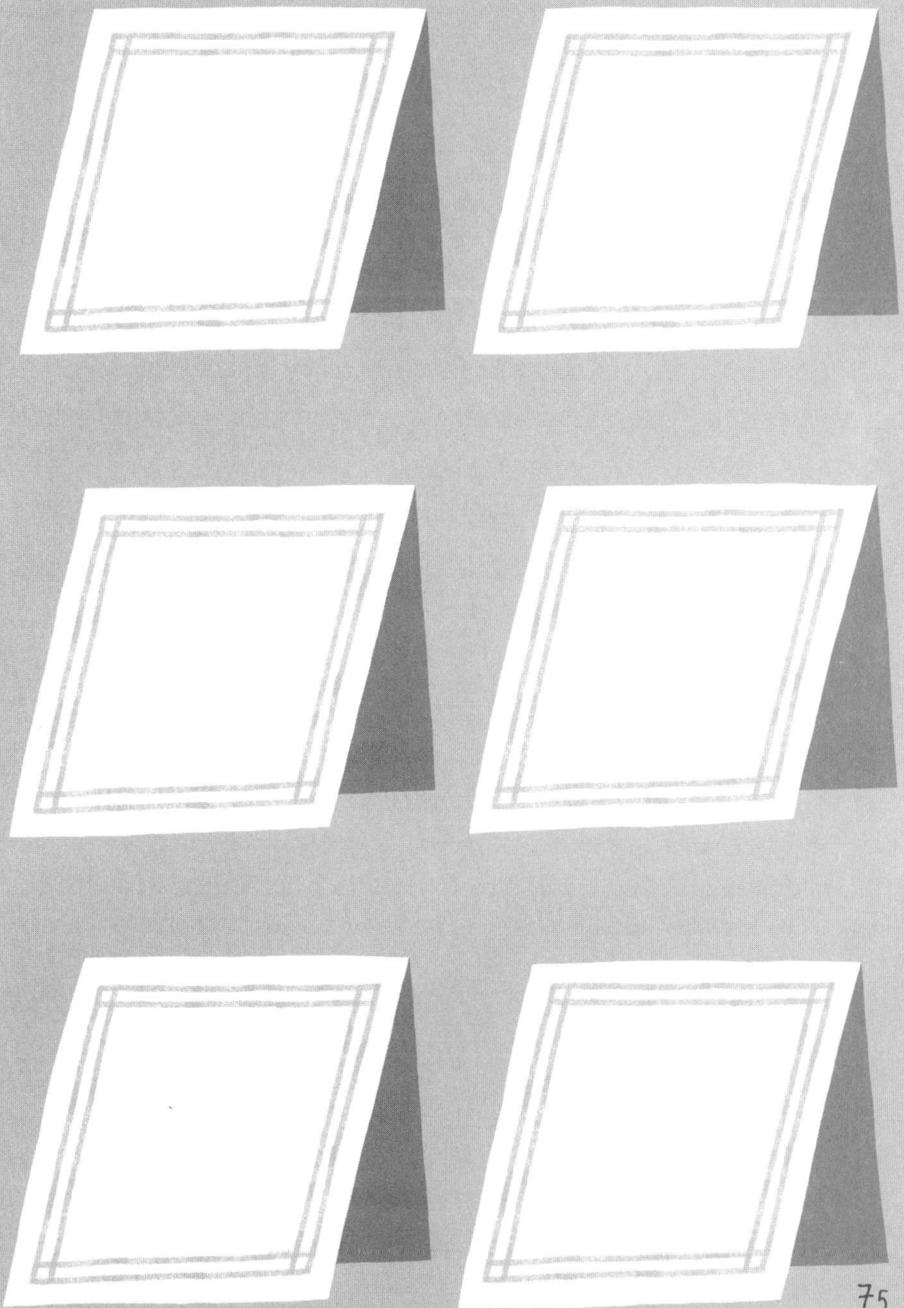

75

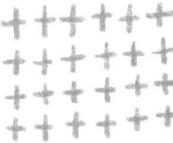

a map of my tender heart — what are the
aches or disappointments that still linger?

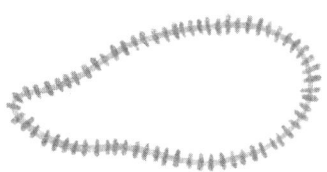

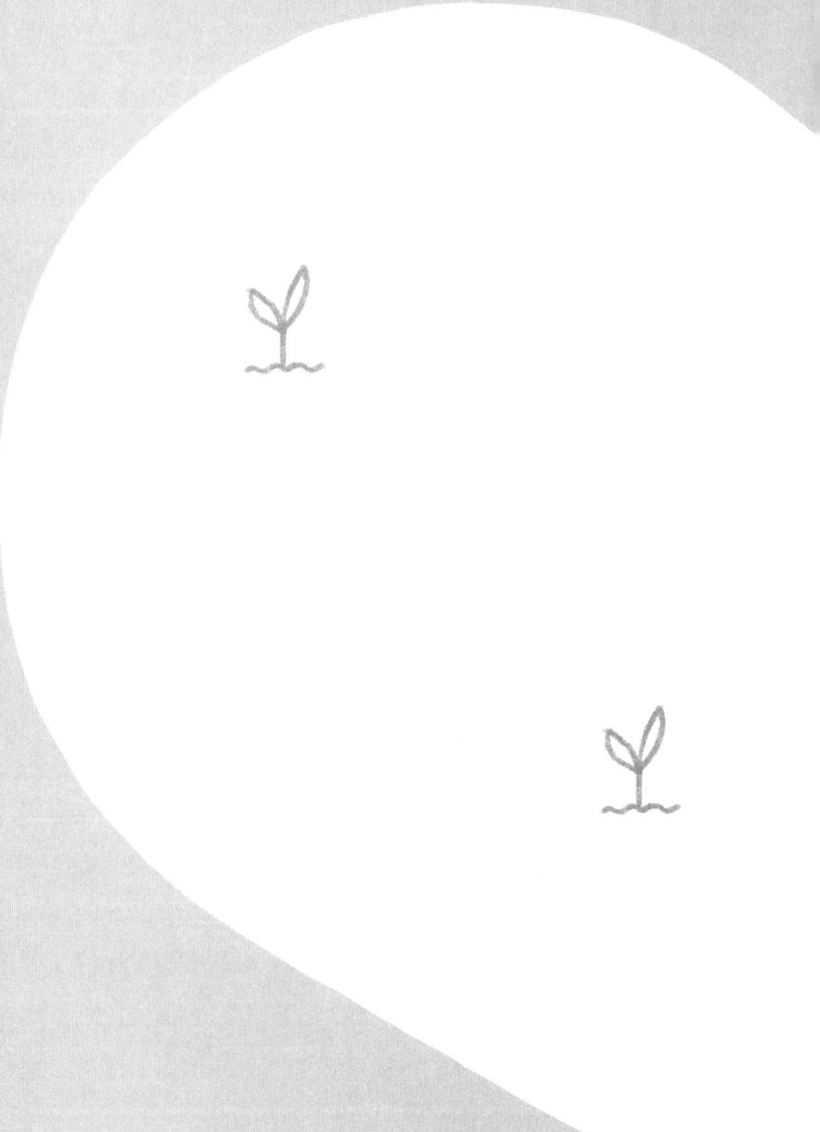

a map of my hopeful heart – what's giving me a tingle of possibility lately?

what are some of the little fireworks
in my heart? times when i felt a spark
of giddy connection with another human,
even if just for the moment.

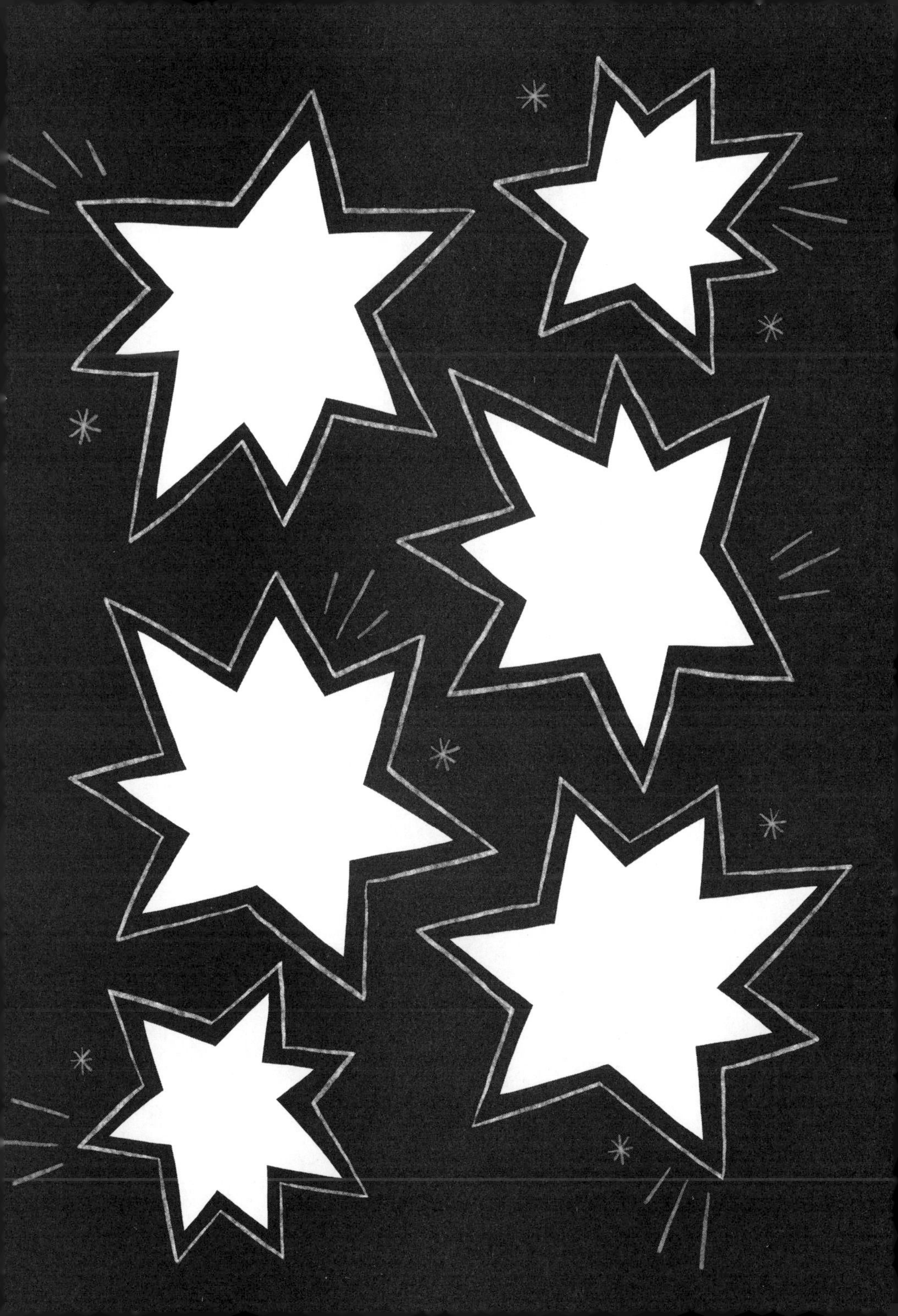

on a first date, are there any questions i dread being asked or conversations that are starting to feel a bit dull to me?

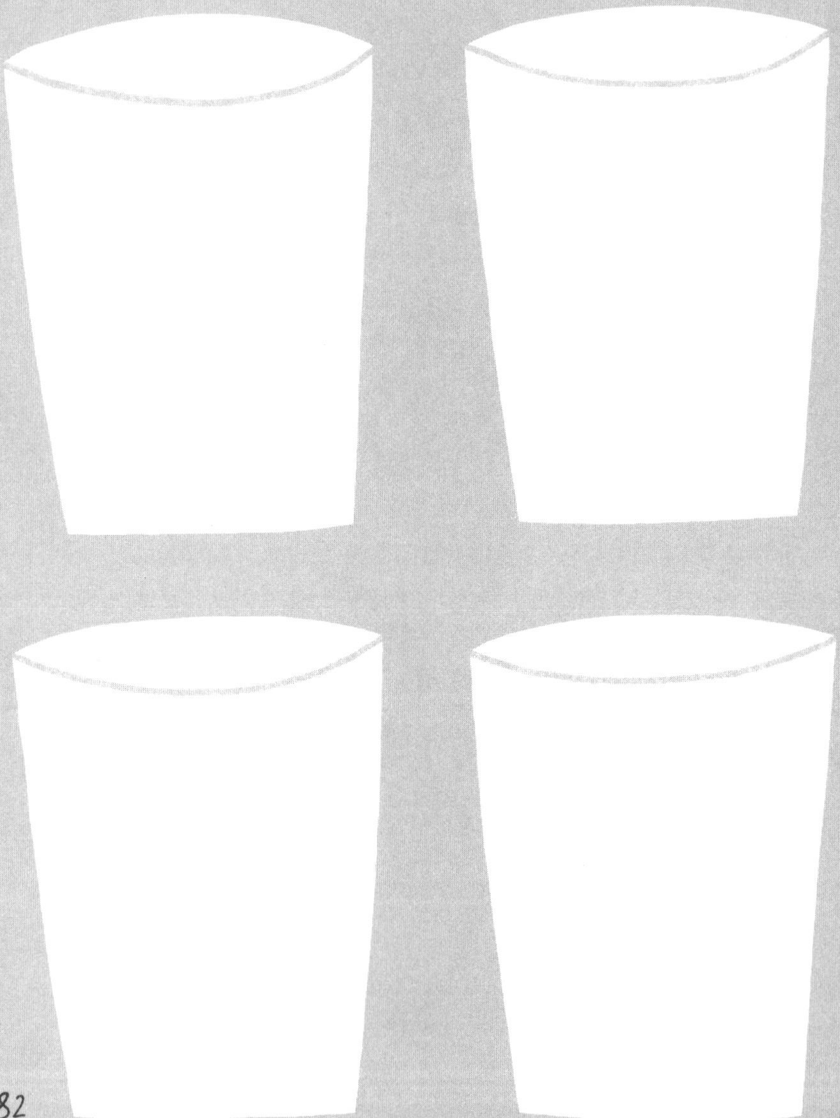

what topics could i happily chat about for hours with the right person? are there any questions i'm craving to ask or be asked?

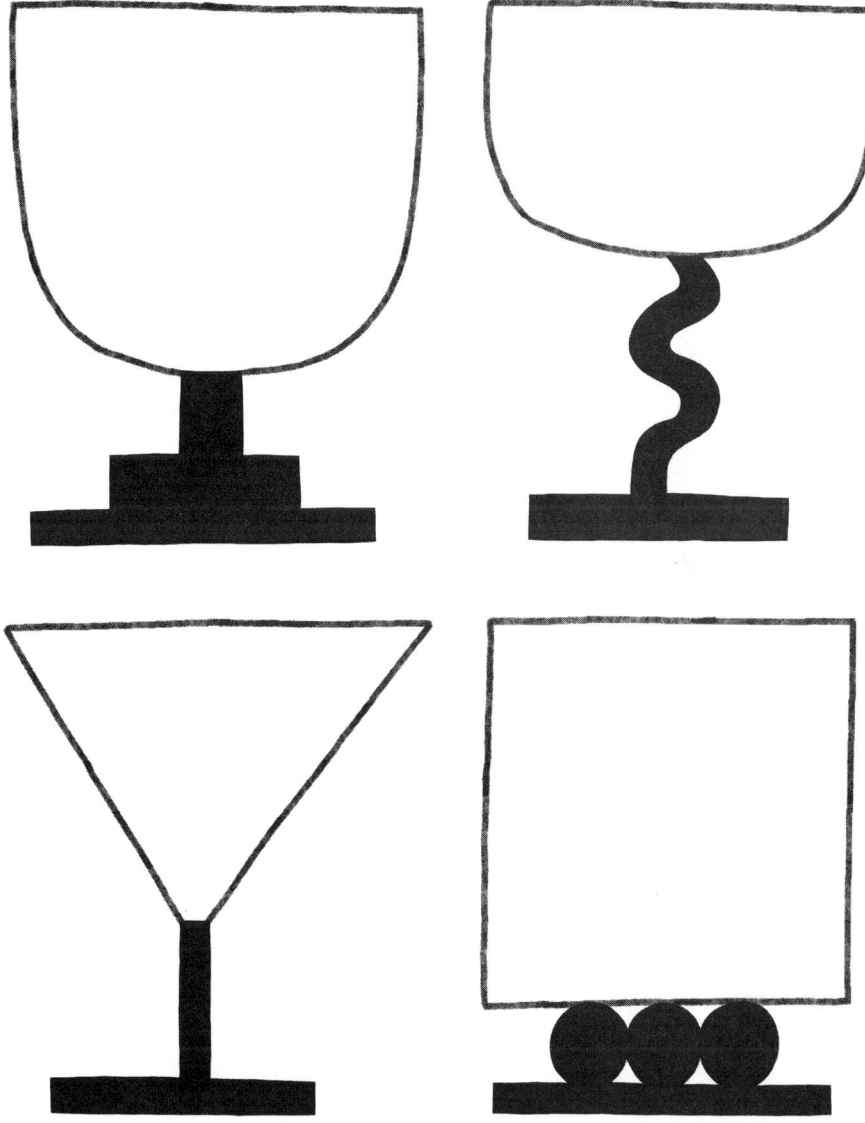

if feelings of rejection & disappointment
arrive at my door, as they sometimes do,
what do i hope my future-self remembers?

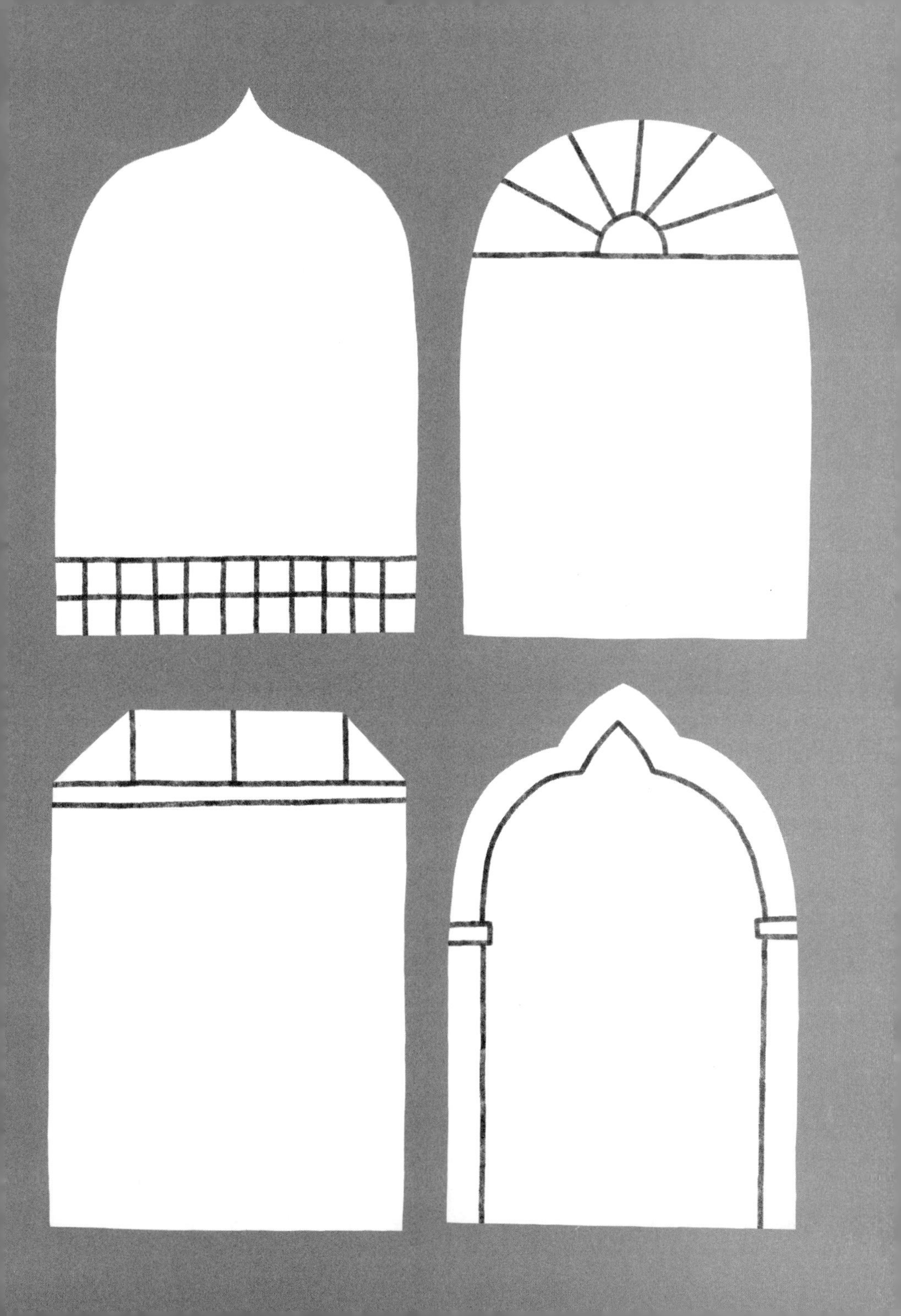

when i start to like someone, what assumptions
do i tend to carry with me from past experiences?
how do i worry things may play out again?

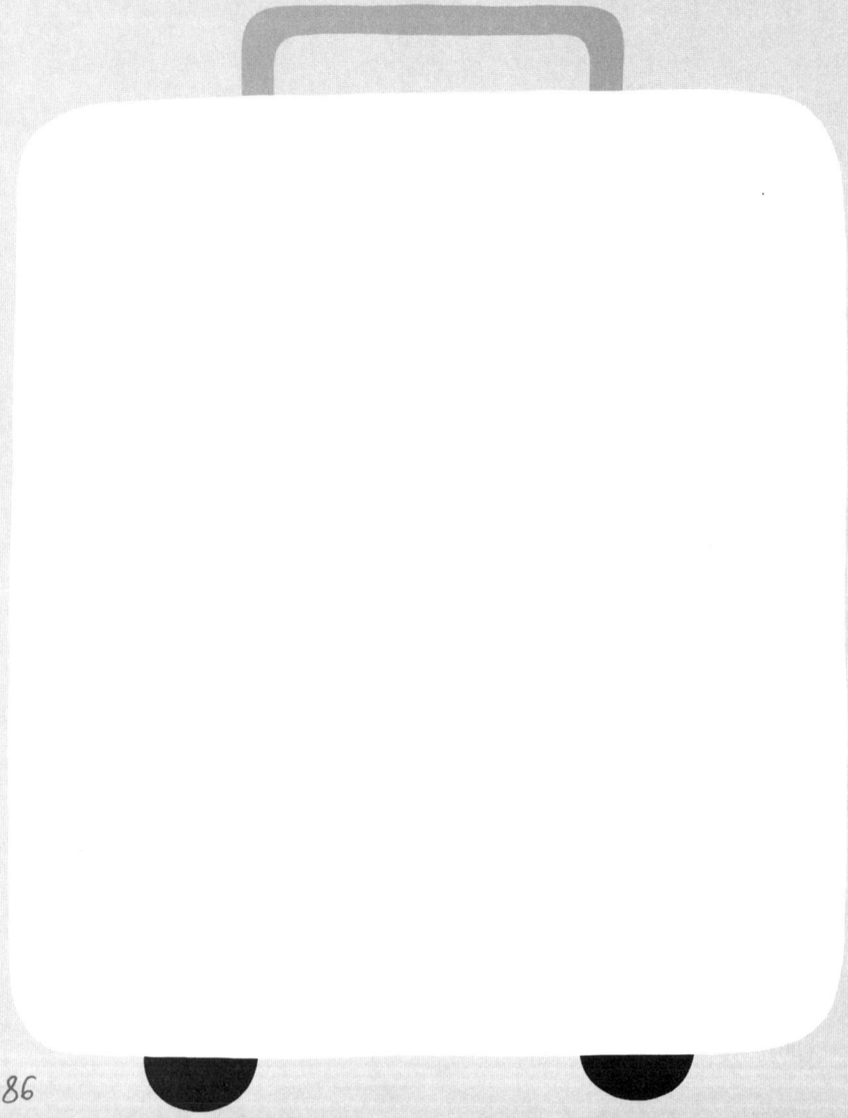

what lighter possibilities might i carry instead? without thinking too far into the future, what could i find in the here & now with someone?

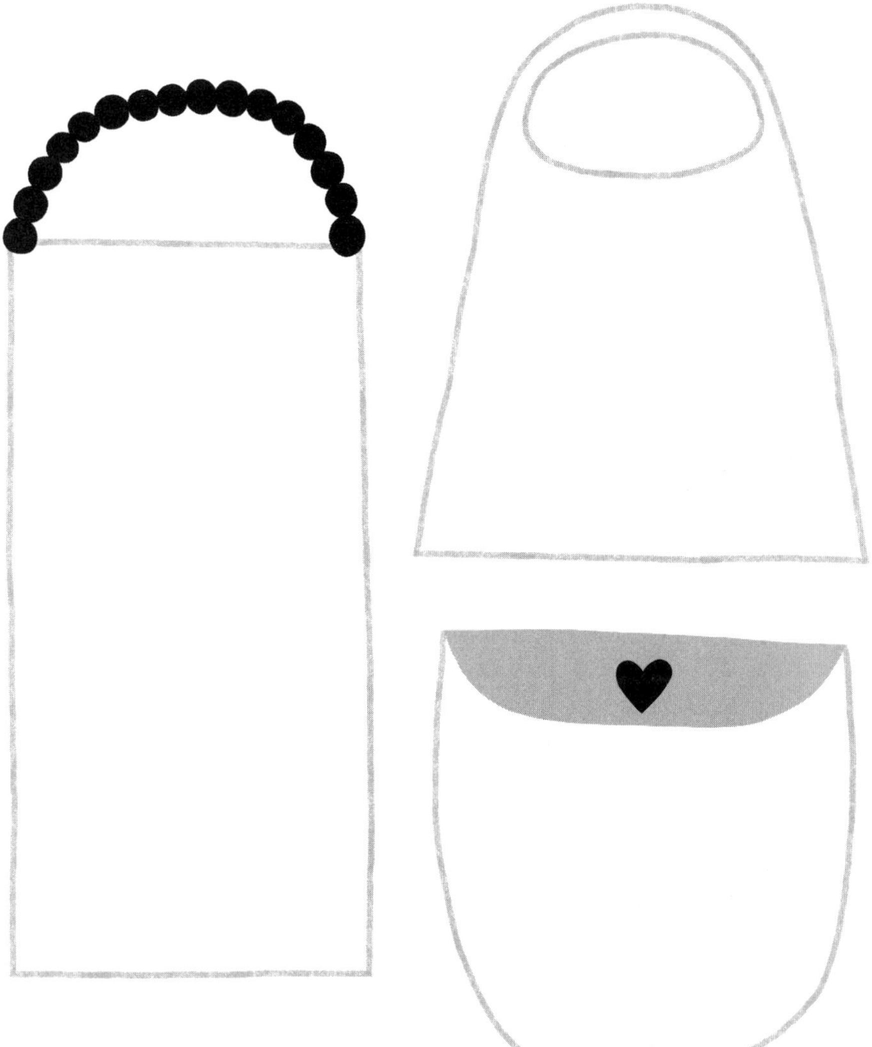

the parts of dating & putting myself
"out there" that i find most drain my battery

the rituals & routines
i can rely on to help me
recharge & feel my best

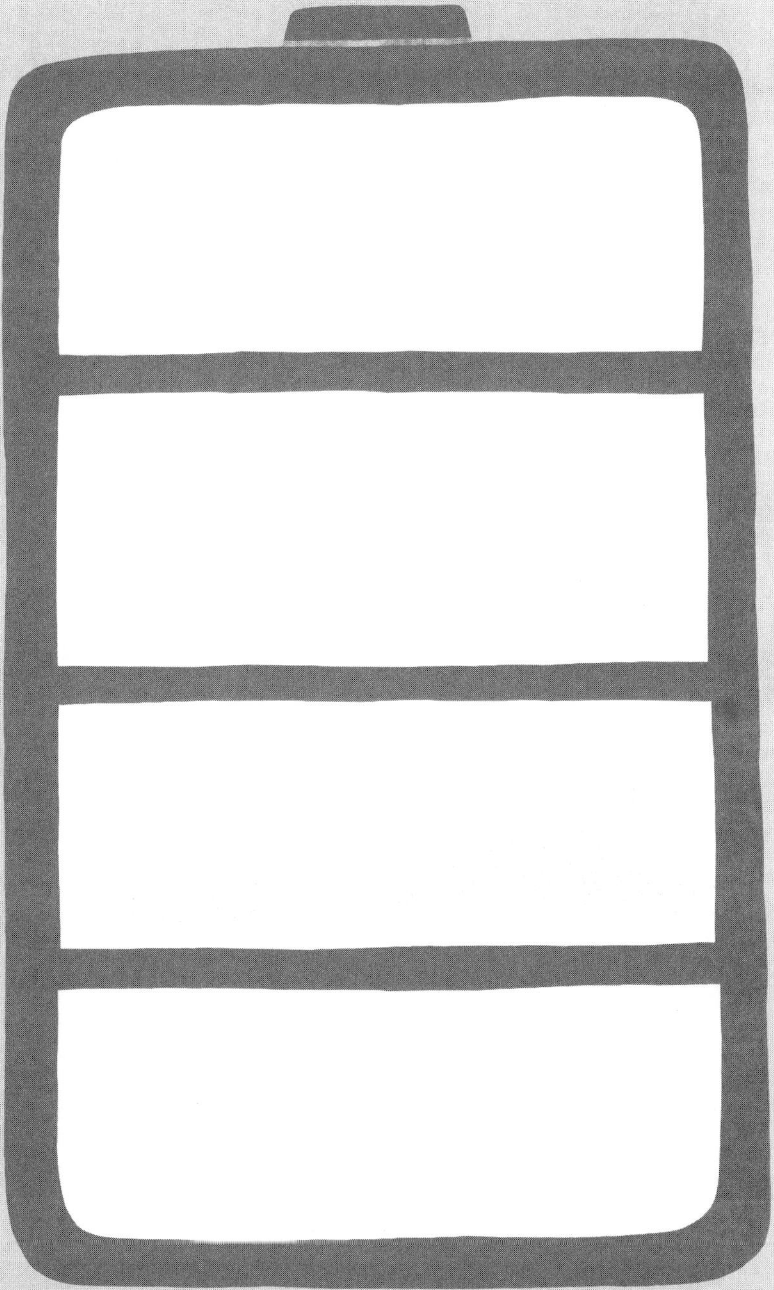

# QUESTIONS TO ASK A TRUSTED FRIEND

what three things do you see in me that you hope anyone i date sees too?

what's one way you
wish a past partner had
treated me better?

what do you hope
i remember before each
date i go on?

dating can feel exhausting at times,
for many reasons: navigating a potential
connection with someone you're yet to
really know. trying to nurture a tender
hope, while also preparing for possible
disappointment. needing to tune in to what
your own heart is saying & wanting to
handle someone else's with care too.

the next few pages are a retreat from
the endless scroll of dating apps. a moment
of analog peace to take a few breaths,
decide to show up & acknowledge yourself
with a flower each time you do.

when you make plans to meet someone,
write their name alongside a flower.

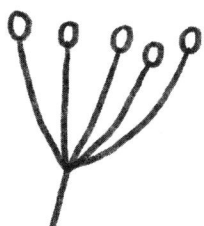

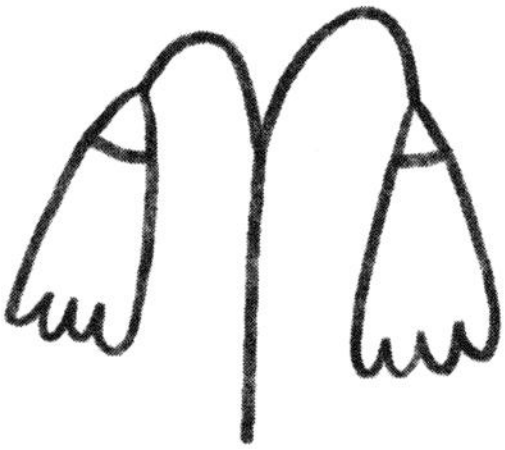

then after you meet,
however it goes, add that
flower to a vase.

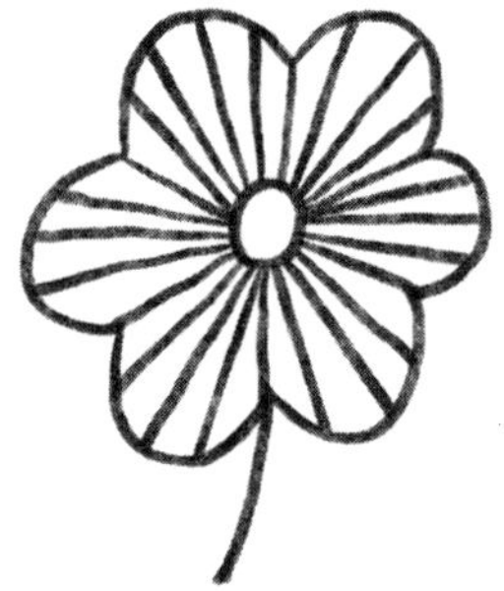

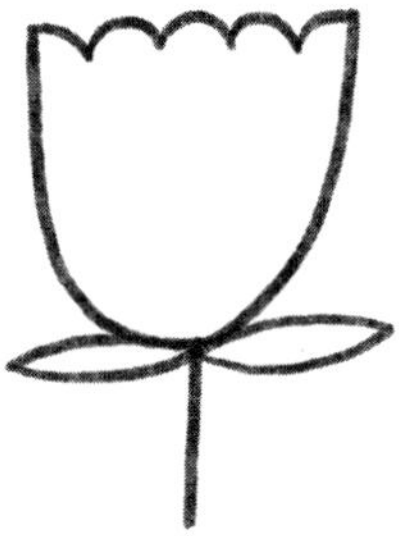

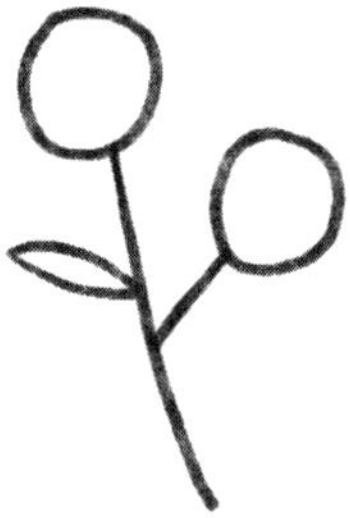

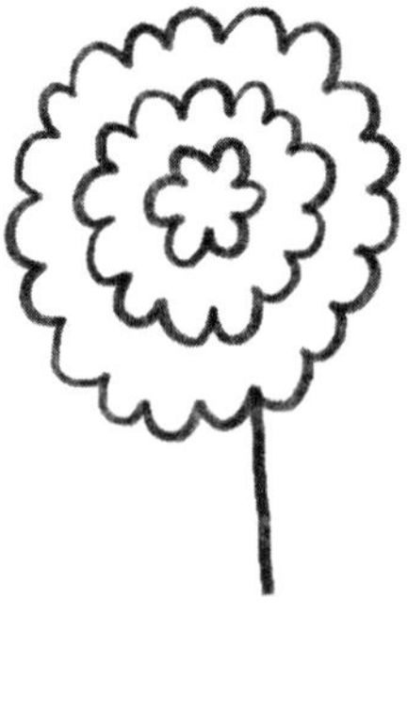

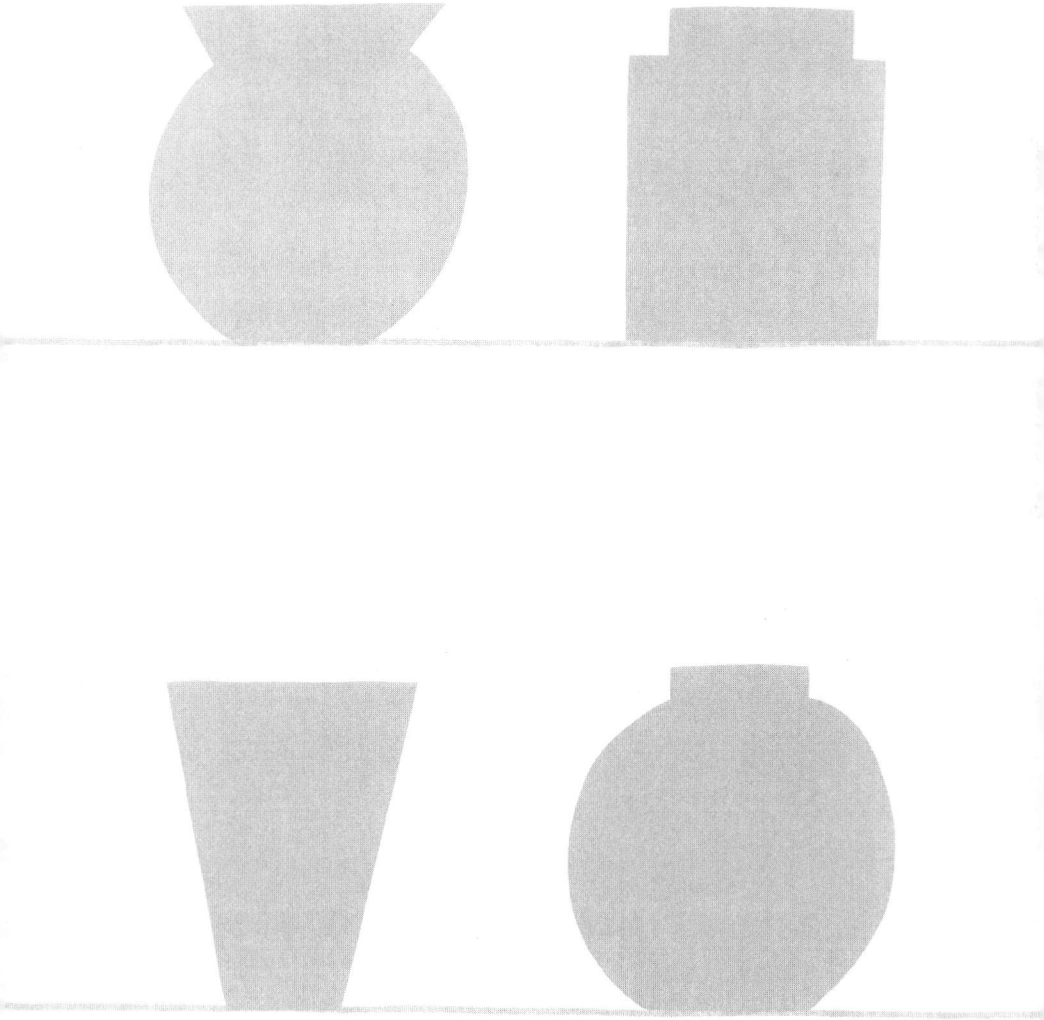

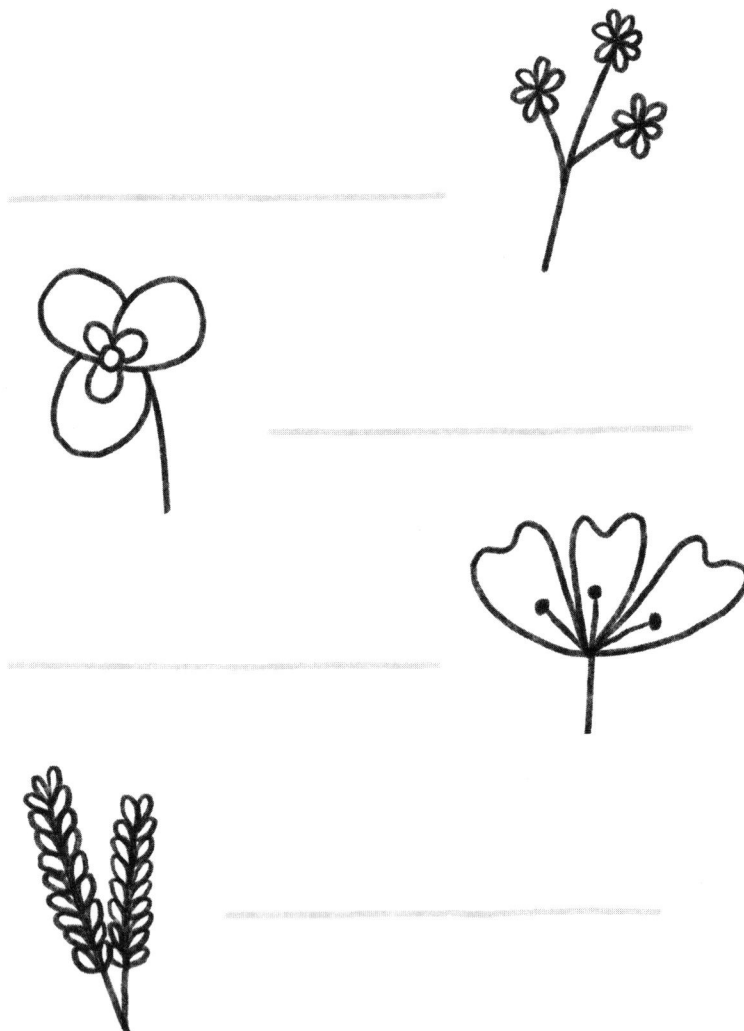

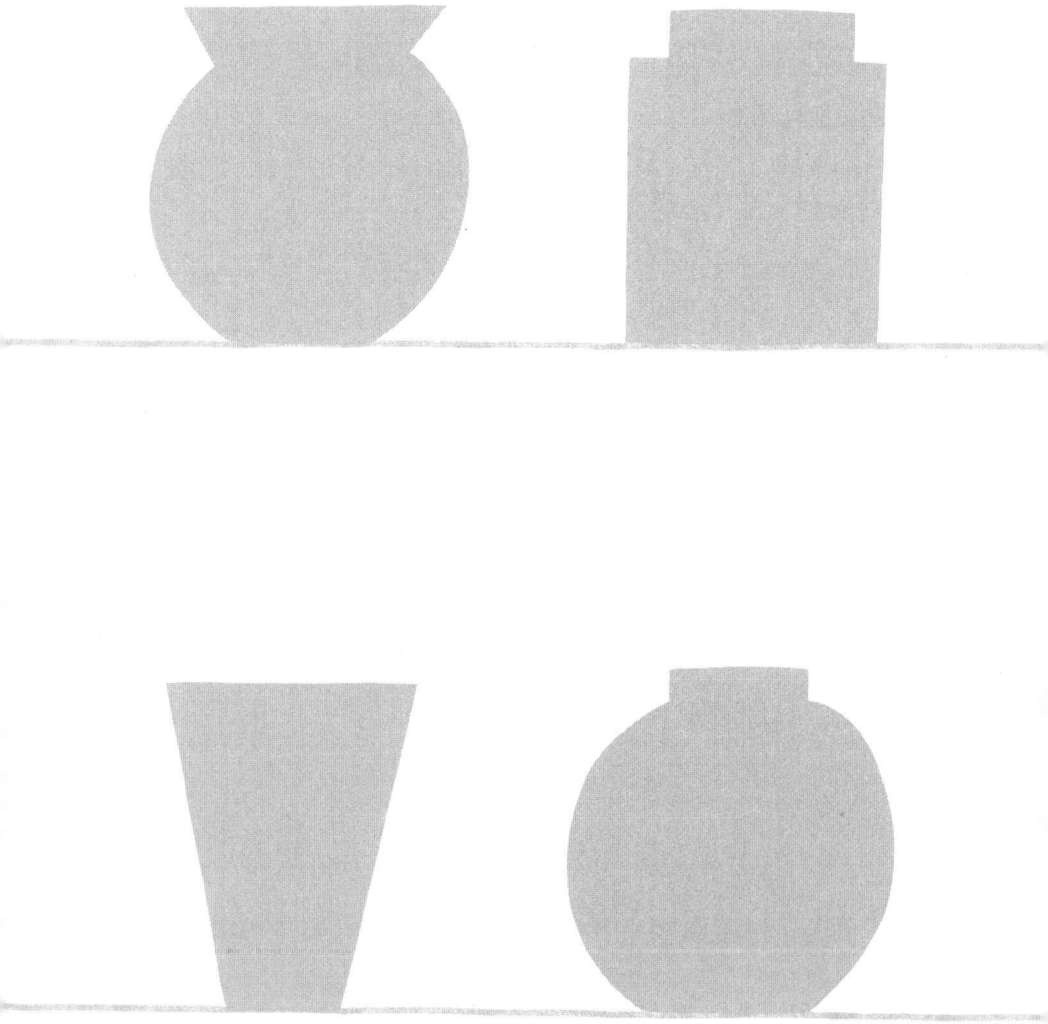

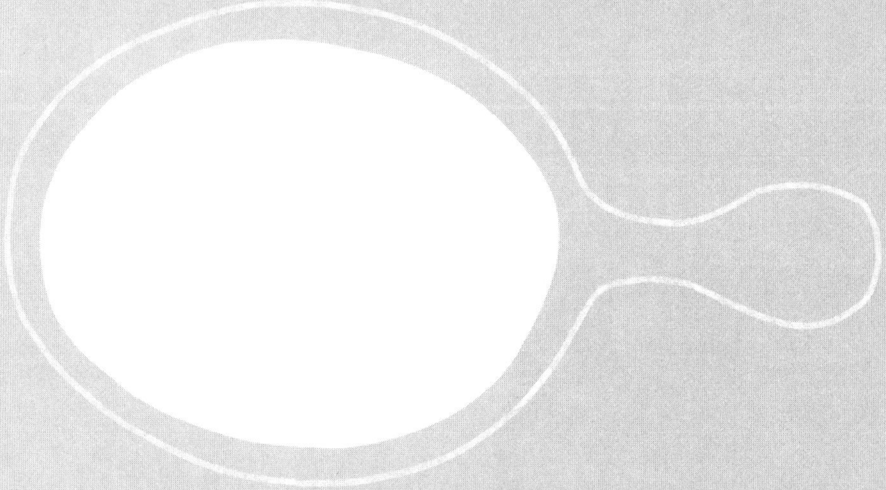

if someone offers a loving reflection
of who i am, what do i hope they say?
what are the parts of myself i need
reaffirmed to feel my best?

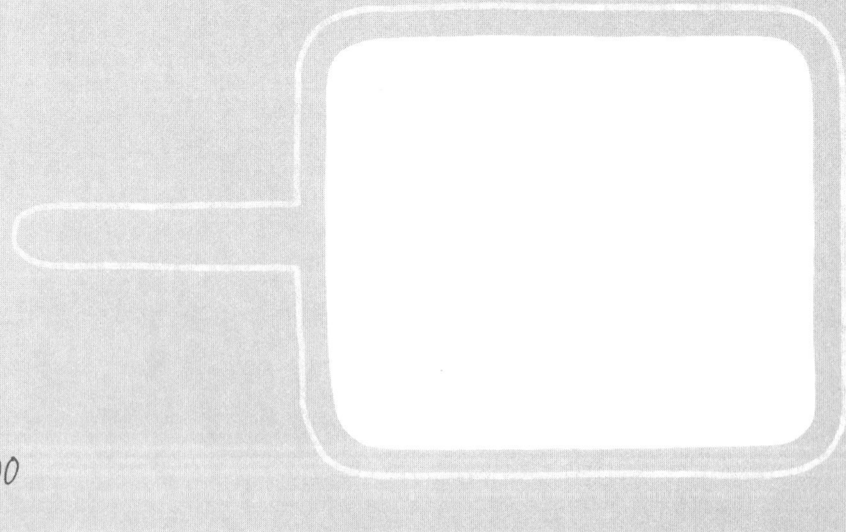

101

encouraging messages from my friends,
saved for eternal use!

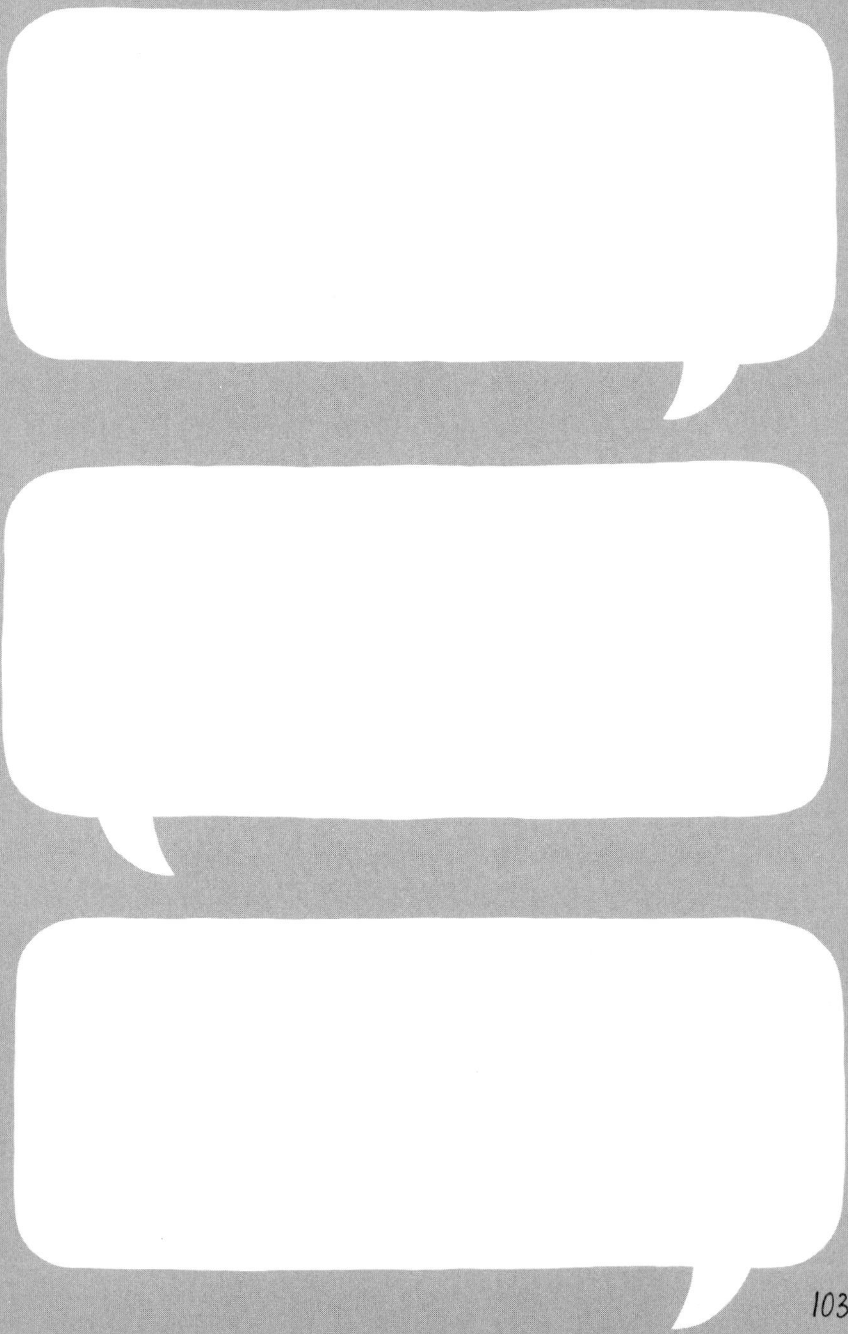

103

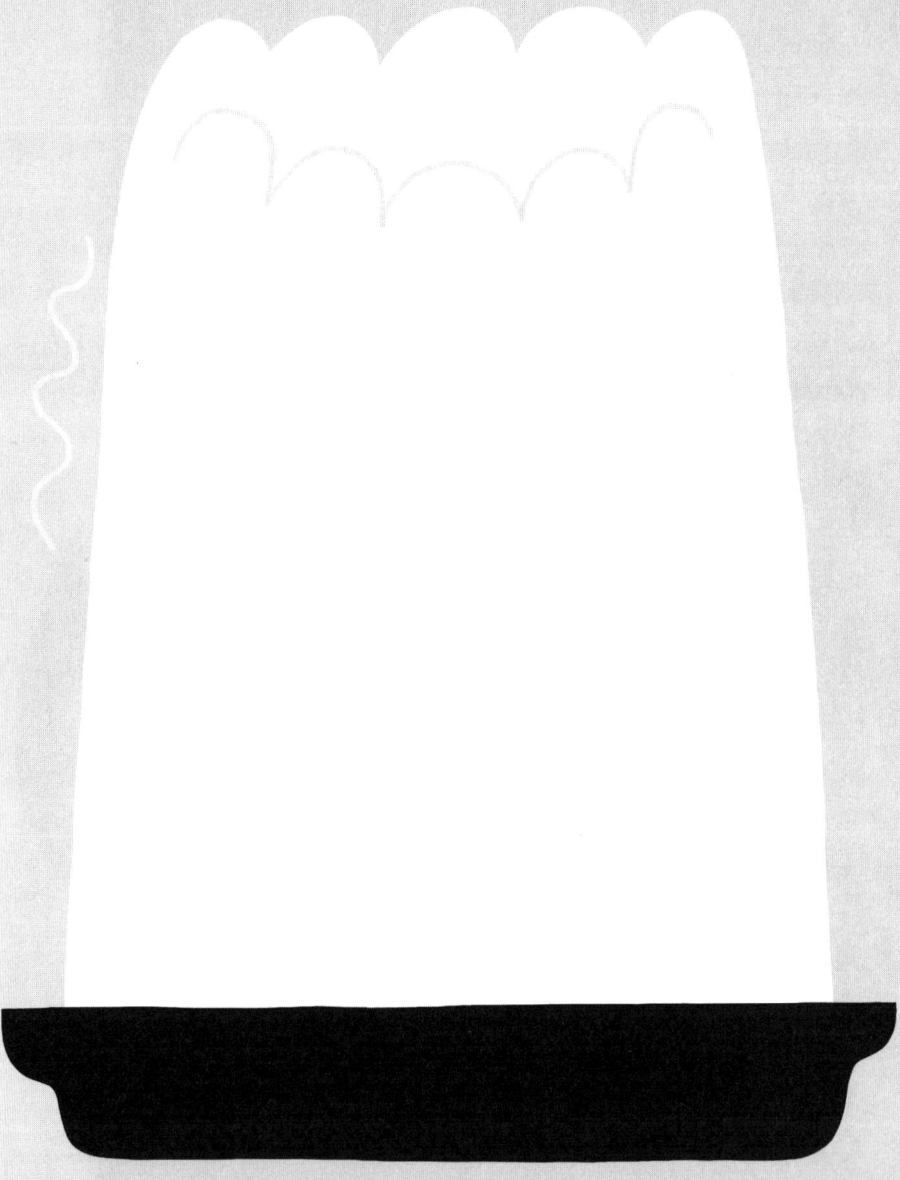

the worries that tend to feed
my first date jitters

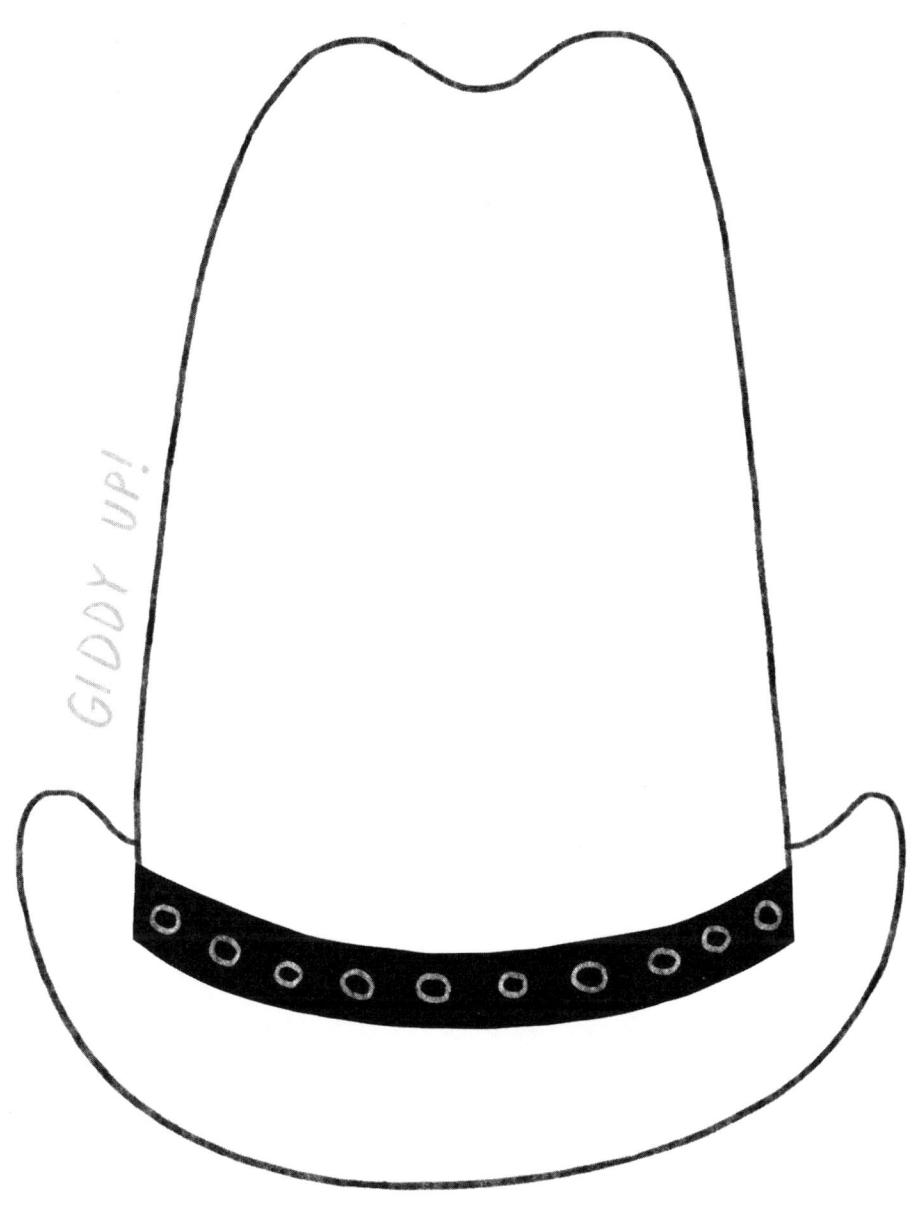

GIDDY UP!

the magic words to get me out the door

SOUVENIRS

this is your space for an easy debrief
after you meet someone new, or after
a second, third or fourth date.

there's no particular order to this chapter.
just flip to a page that feels fitting & leave
a little memento of your time together. give
yourself some closure after a date, if that's
what you're needing, or savor some sweetness
when you find it, even if it's fleeting.

when your mind is only on the end goal,
dating can be an exhausting cycle of
hope & deflation. maybe these debriefs can
shift your focus a little so you can see
dating for what it also is — life in the now.

a tiny moment of
connection with

unexpected places the conversation traveled to with

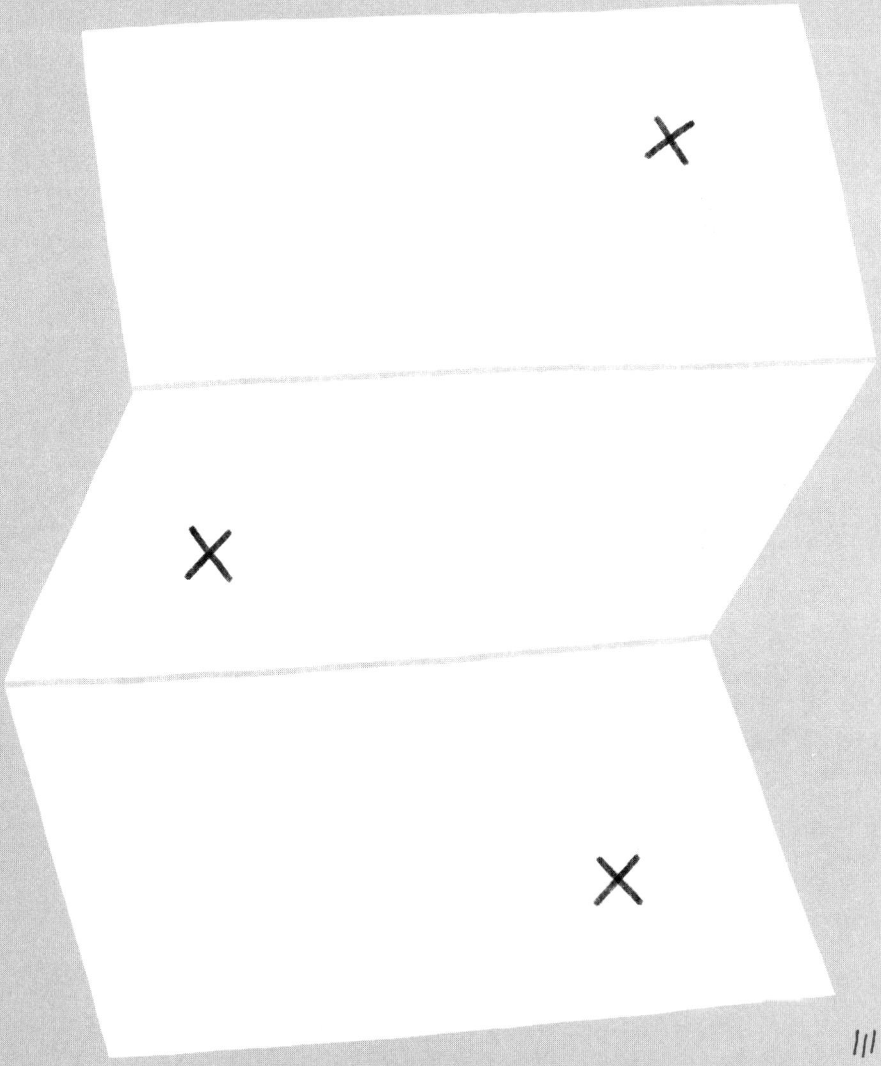

what surprised me most
as i got to know

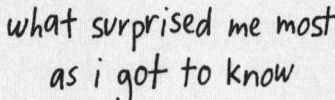

the soundtrack of
my time spent with

the shared passion
i found with

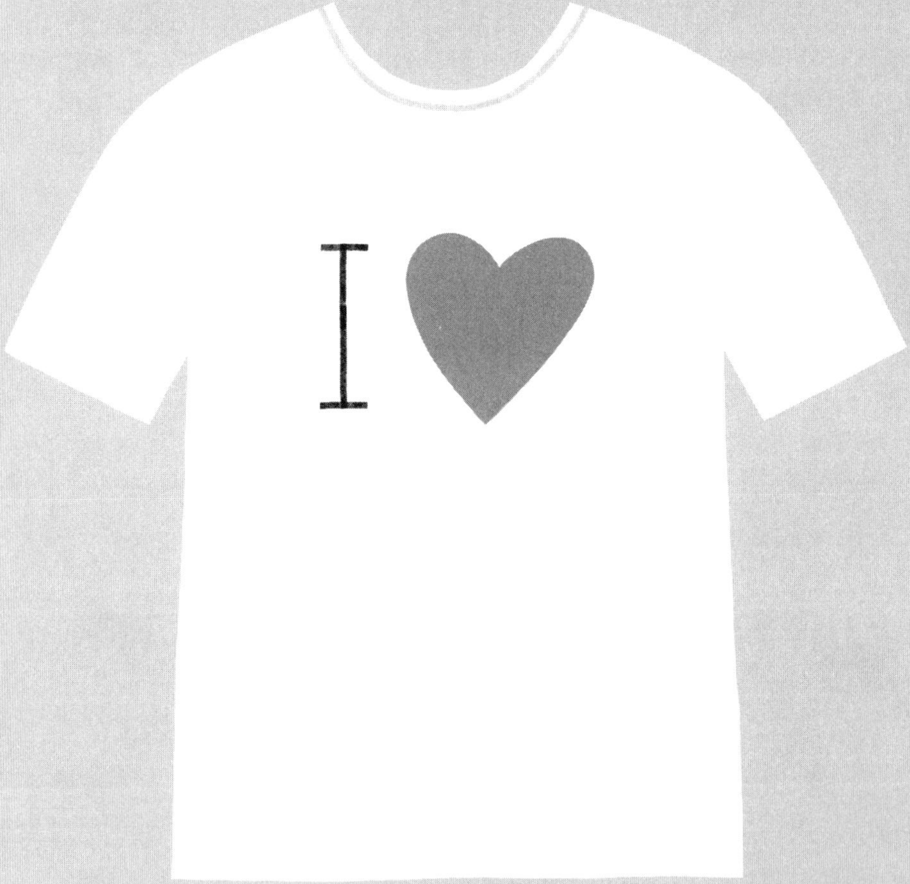
I

a scent to remind me
of my date with

what i'm daydreaming about
after my date with

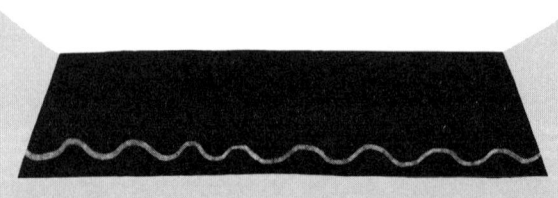

why i feel it's just not
the right match with

117

the expectation & the reality
of my date with

the exact moment i felt
an attraction to

where we each took the
lead on my date with

the plan i cooked up with

(that may or may not ever happen!)

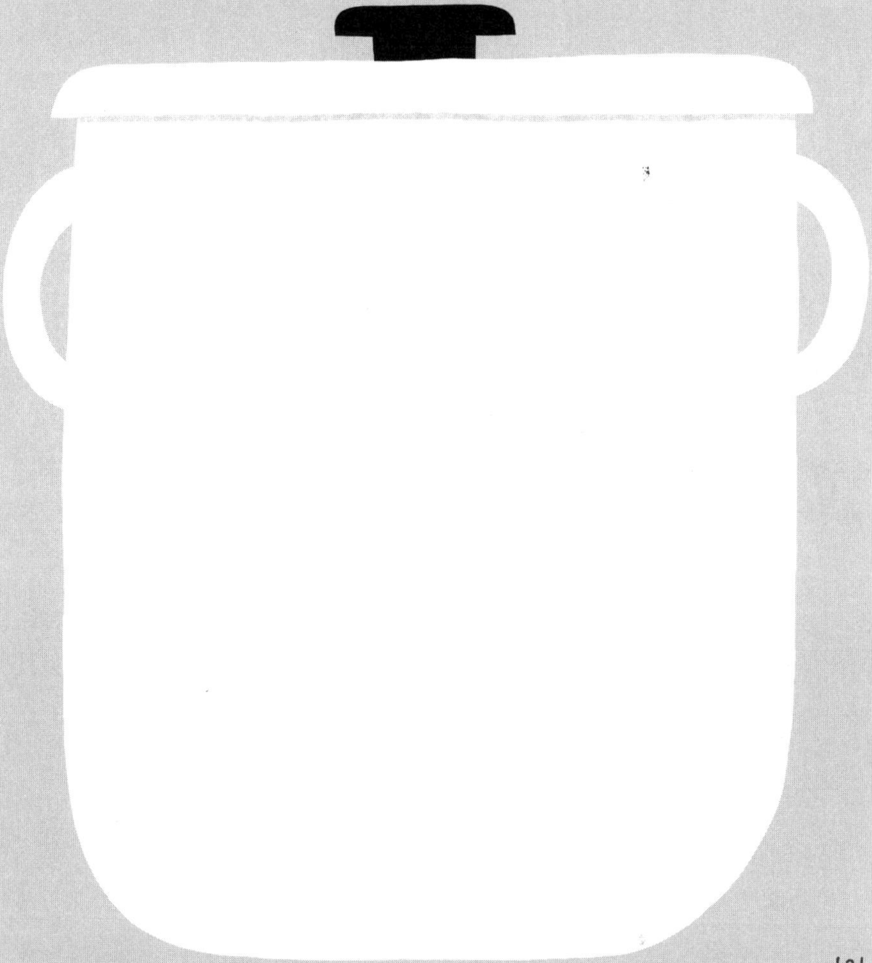

a little celebration
i got to share with

at least it was a good story!
my date with

Once

a whole new world
i was shown by

what first caught my attention
on my date with

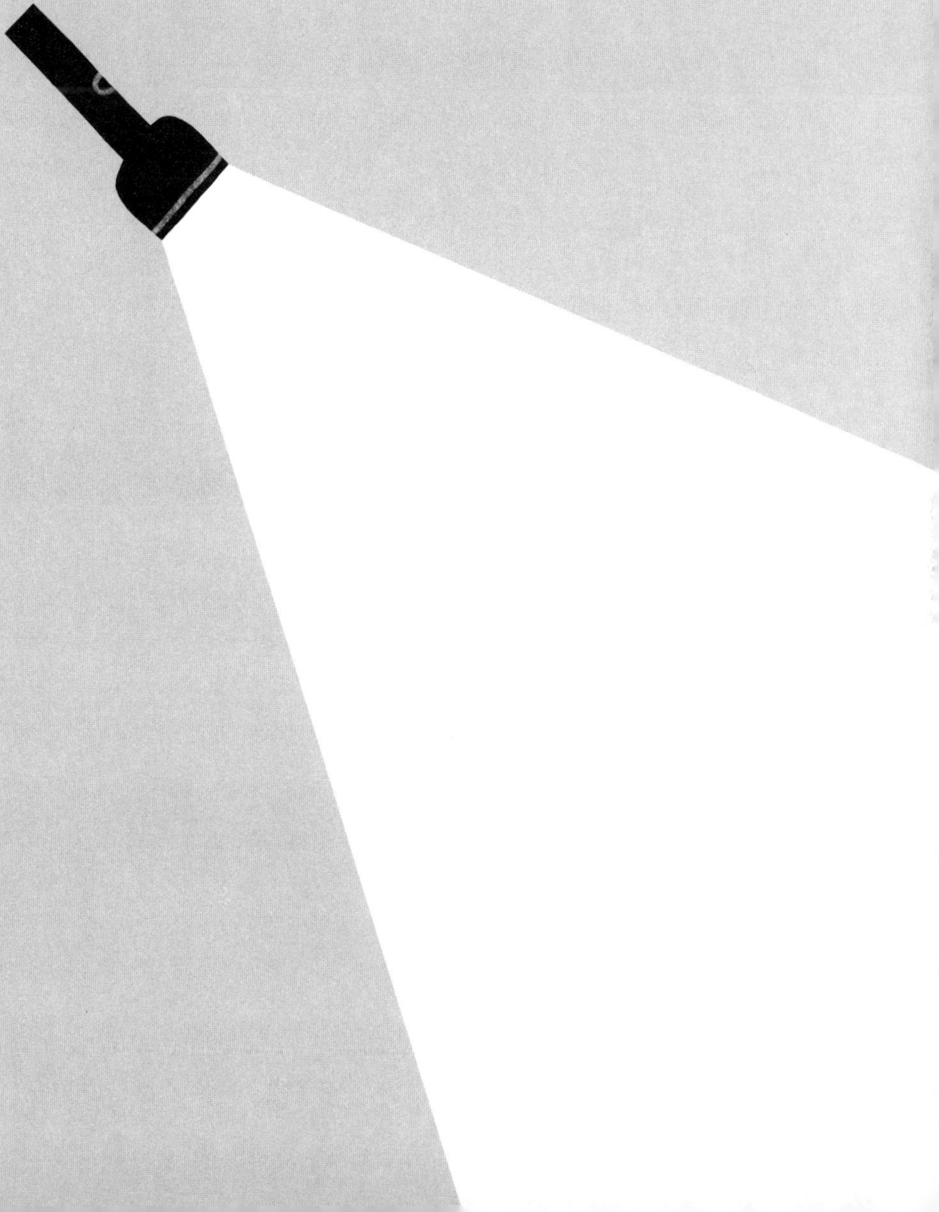

if our conversation was a house,
all the rooms i visited with

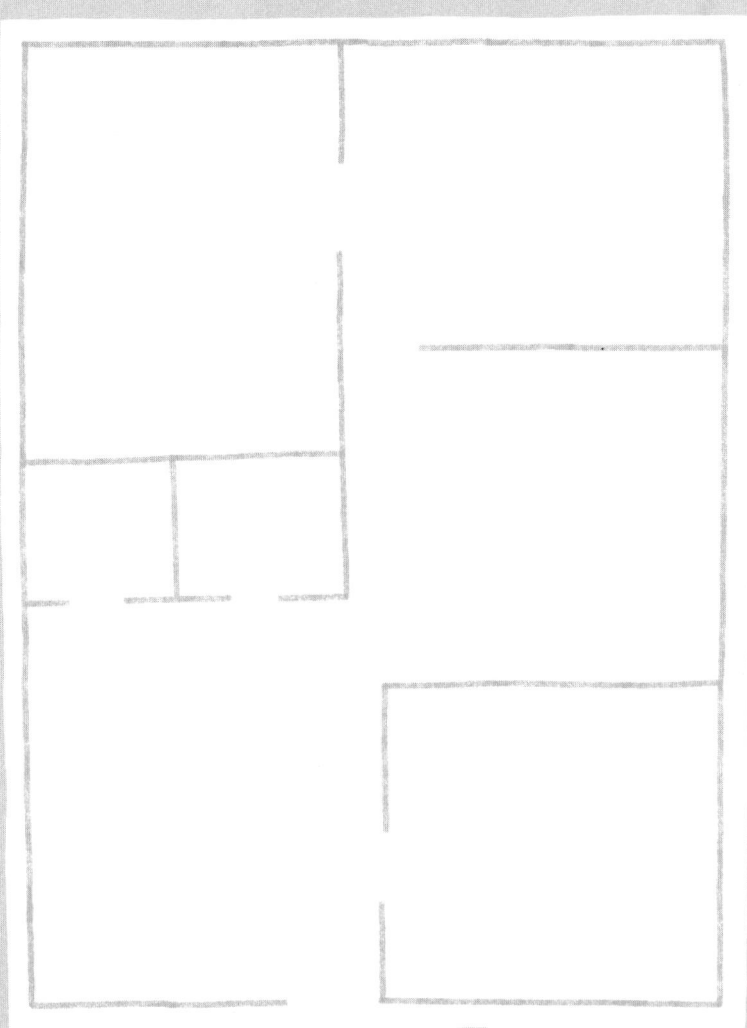

my first impression
& a closer observation of

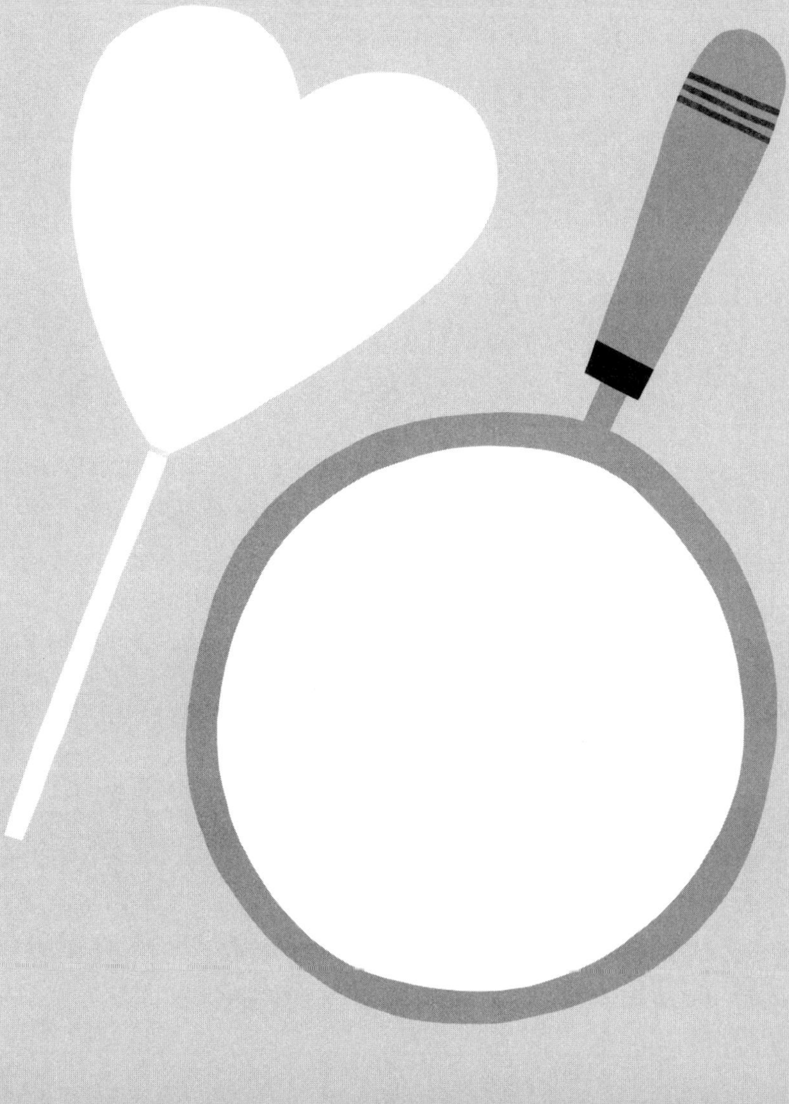

the behavior i chose not
to tolerate from

where it led when i followed
the thread of desire with

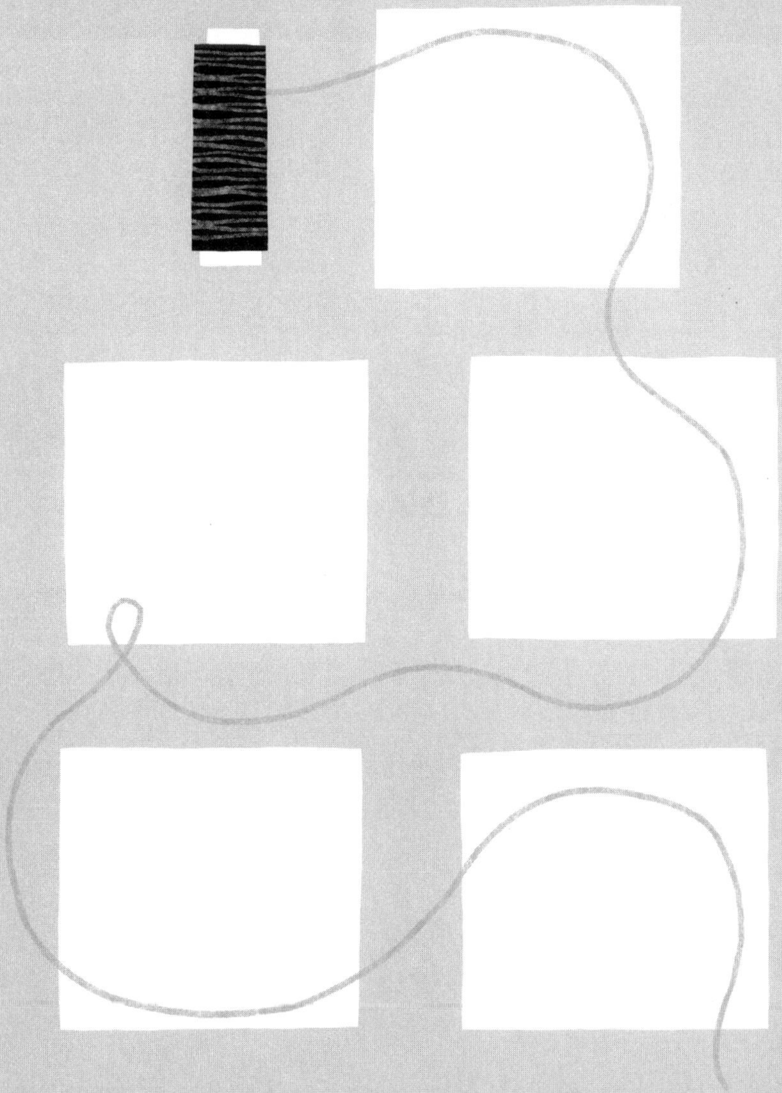

possibilities on my mind
as i spent time with

the words i wanted
to whisper to

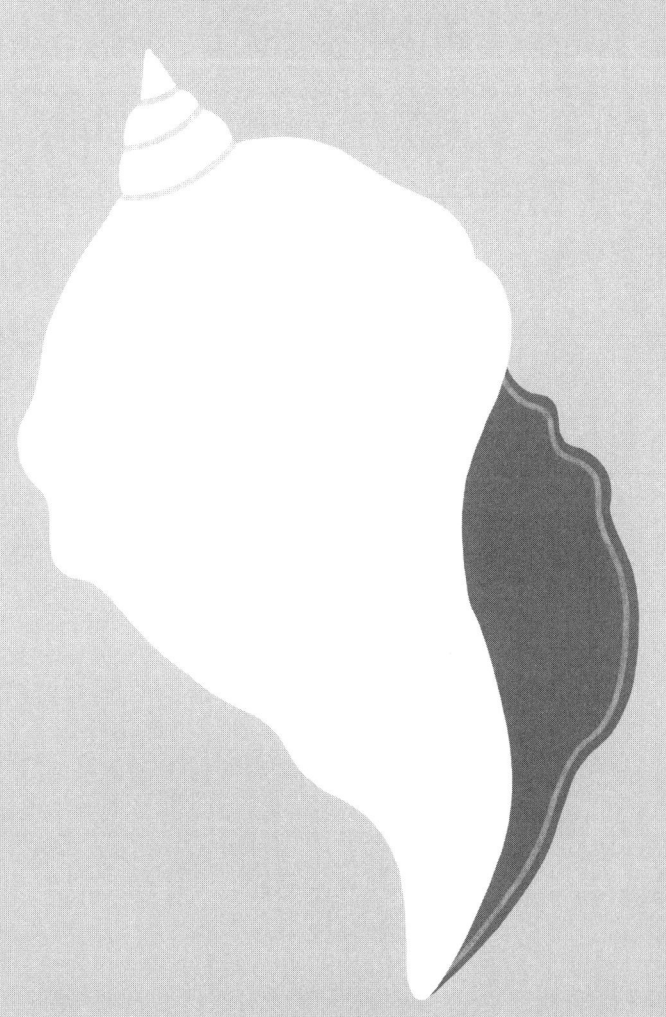

where things went sour
on my date with

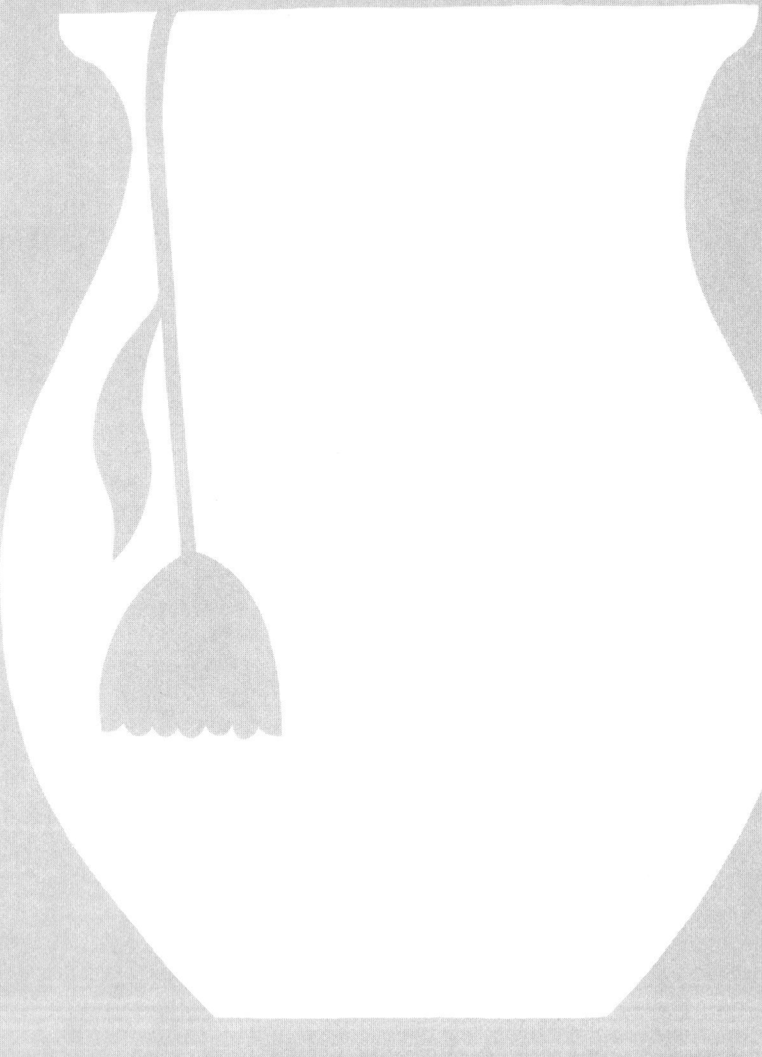

a moment of warmth
i appreciated from

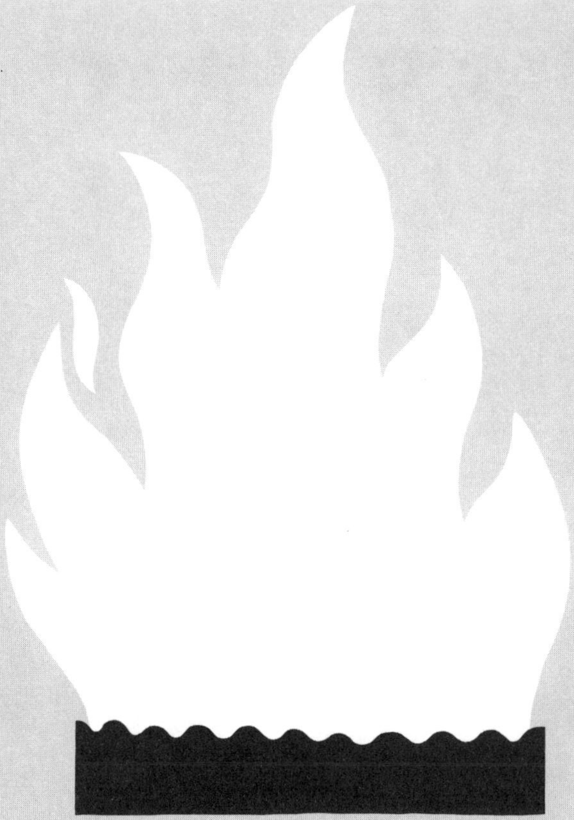

an excellent suggestion from

how my date began
& where it ended up with

135

things i'm curious to learn more about after spending time with

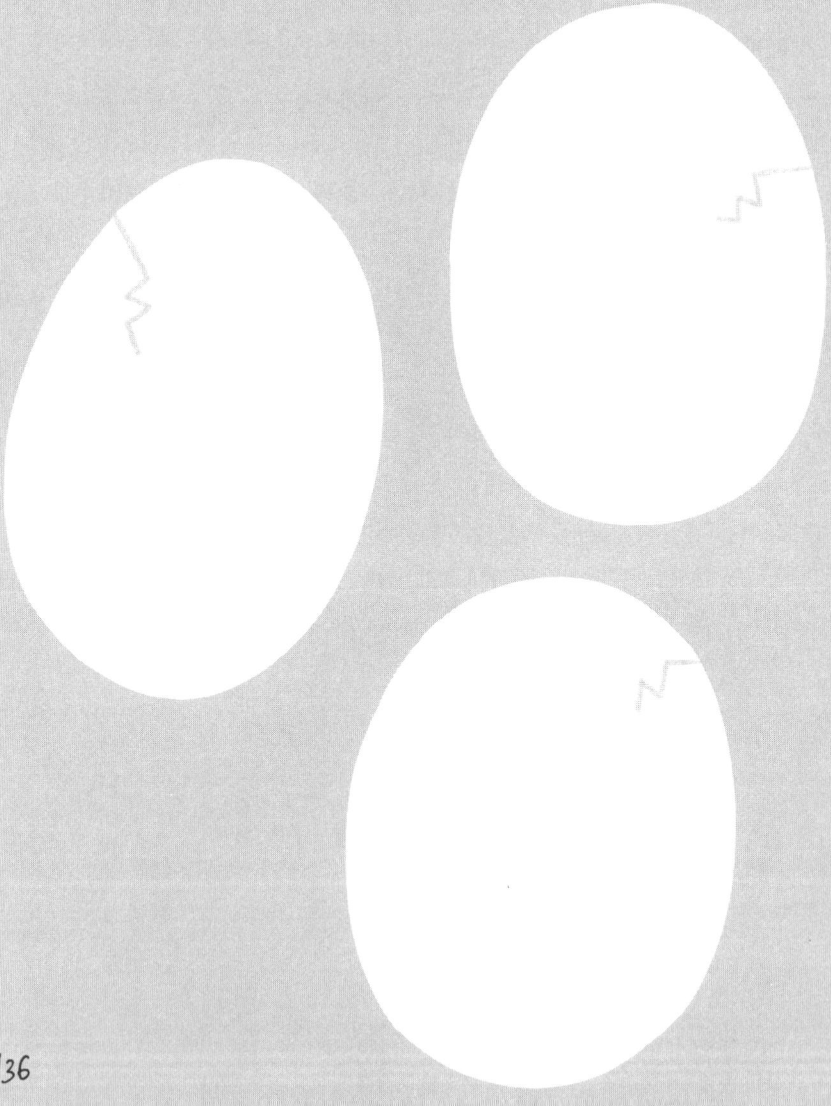

how i felt about myself
when i was with

the turn-on i didn't know
i had until i met

where the winds took us
on my date with

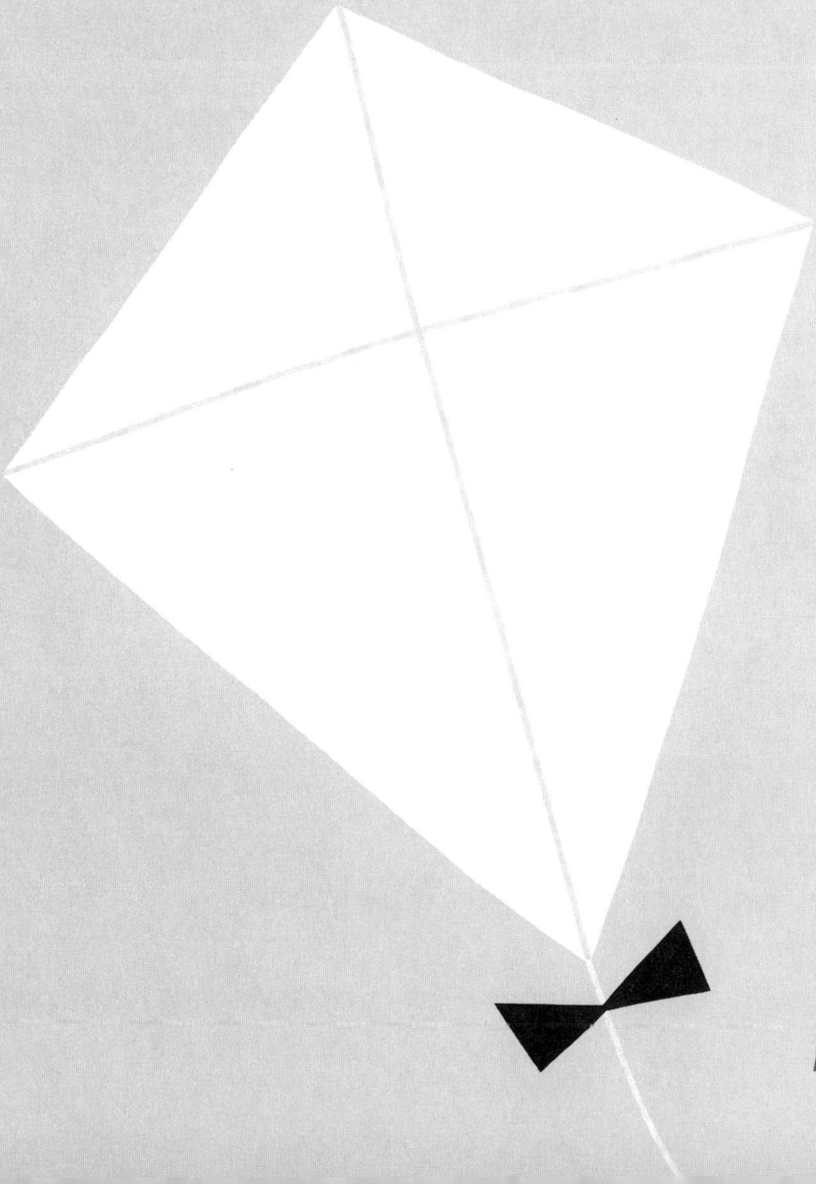

what i was curious to find
when i got a peek into the life of

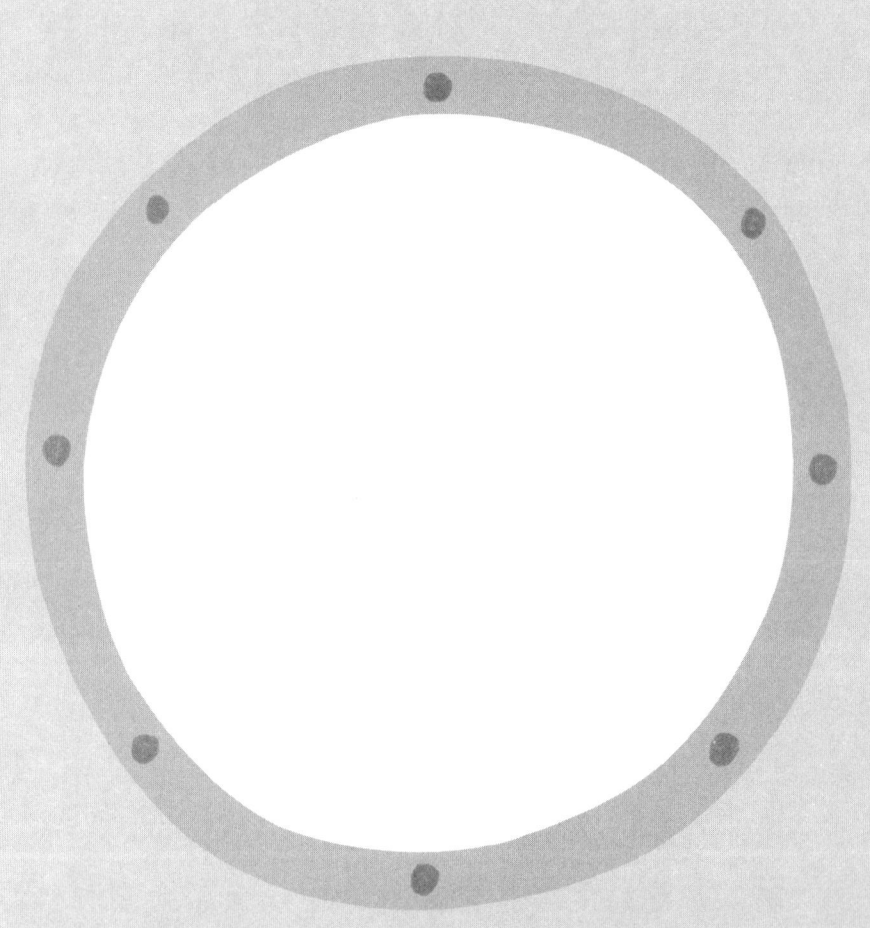

the heart-to-heart
chat i shared with

what felt like a sign of
good luck when i met

what i was happy to come
home to after my date with

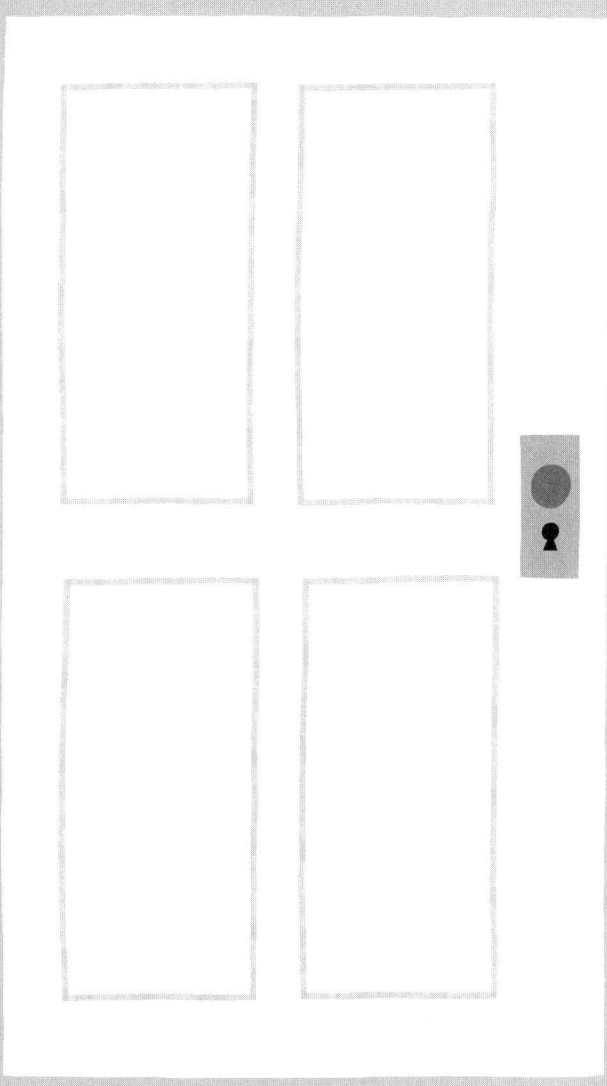

# NOTES

# NOTES

# NOTES

# NOTES

a special thanks to

marian & the team at TarcherPerigee,
for your keen eyes & kindness;

Sorche, for your constant & evolving
support over the years;

Sara, my cuz, for your friendship.

photo by Tatanja Ross

Lisa Currie (b. 1987) is an Australian author
& illustrator living in her hometown of
melbourne/Naarm. her pages are a playful
space to connect with a loved one or gently
untangle what's on your mind right now.

for more, visit lisacurrie.com

other books by Lisa Currie

"Guidebook to the Unknown"
is a journal for anxious minds

"Notes to Self"
is a journal for self-care

"Surprise Yourself"
is a creative playbook to get out
of your head & into the world

"The Positivity Kit"
is instant happiness on every page!

the "me, You, Us" series
are books to fill out together
with your friends or a loved one

"The Scribble Diary"
is your daily doodling space